THE TRANSFORMATION OF DEMOCRACY

COLLEGE FOR HUMAN SERVICES
LIBRARY
345 HUDSON STREET
NEW YORK, N.Y. 10014

Social Science Classics Series

Vilhelm Aubert, *The Hidden Society*
Samuel Bernstein, *French Political and Intellectual History*
Herbert Blumber, *Critiques of Research in the Social Sciences*
G.S. Churye, *The Scheduled Tribes of India*
G.D.H. Cole, *Guild Socialism Restated*
Charles Horton Cooley, *Human Nature and the Social Order*
Charles Horton Cooley, *Social Organization*
Benedetto Croce, *Historical Materialism and the Economics of Karl Marx*
Albert Venn Dicey, *Lectures on the Relation between Law and Public Opinion in England during the Nineteenth Century*
Adam Ferguson, *An Essay on the History of Civil Society*
Ludwig Gumplowicz, *Outlines of Sociology*
Everett C. Hughes, *The Sociological Eye*
Helen MacGill Hughes, *News and the Human Interest Story*
Kurt Koffka, *Growth of the Mind*
Walter Laqueur, *Young Germany*
Harold J. Laski, *The American Presidency*
Gustave LeBon, *The French Revolution and the Psychology of Revolution*
Gustave LeBon, *The Psychology of Socialism*
Walter Lippman, *A Preface to Morals*
Helen Merril Lynd, *England in the Eighteen-Eighties*
Harriet Martineau, *Society in America*
Vilfredo Pareto, *The Transformation of Democracy*
Joseph A. Schumpeter, *The Theory of Economic Development*
George Bernard Shaw, *The Intelligent Woman's Guide to Socialism*
Werner Sombart, *The Jews and Modern Capitalism*
Anselm Strauss et al., *Psychiatric Ideologies*
William Graham Sumner, *Earth-Hunger and Other Essays*
Thorstein Veblen, *The Engineers and the Price System*
Thorstein Veblen, *The Theory of Business Enterprise*
Graham Wallas, *Human Nature in Politics*
Max Weber, *General Economic History*
Floran Znaniecki, *Cultural Sciences*

THE TRANSFORMATION OF DEMOCRACY

VILFREDO PARETO

Edited with an Introduction by
Charles H. Powers

Translated by
Renata Girola

Transaction Books
New Brunswick (U.S.A.) and London (U.K.)

Copyright © 1984 by Transaction, Inc.
New Brunswick, New Jersey 08903

All rights reserved under International and Pan-American Copyright Conventions. No part of this book may be reproduced or transmitted in any form or by any means, electronic or mechanical, including photocopy, recording, or any information storage and retrieval system, without prior permission in writing from the publisher. All inquiries should be addressed to Transaction Books, Rutgers—The State University, New Brunswick, New Jersey 08903.

Library of Congress Catalog Number: 83-18089
ISBN: 0-87855-949-3 (paper)
Printed in the United States of America

Library of Congress Cataloging in Publication Data

Pareto, Vilfredo, 1848–1923.
　The transformation of democracy.

　(Social science classics series)
　Translation of: Trasformazione della democrazia.
　Includes bibliographical references and index.
　1. Democracy.　I. Powers, Charles H.　II. Title.
JC423.P25313　1984　　　　　321.8　　　　　　　83-18089
ISBN 0-87855-949-3 (pbk.)

To Jonathan Turner
social physicist

Table of Contents

Editor's Note	ix
Acknowledgments	x
Introduction: The Life and Times of Vilfredo Pareto *Charles H. Powers*	1
1. Generalizations	25
2. The Crumbling of Central Authority	37
3. The Plutocratic Cycle	55
4. Sentiments	63
5. Appendix	73
Epilogue *Charles H. Powers*	87
Index	89

Editor's Note

Developing an accurate translation of any work poses monumental problems. The difficulties are clear when one thinks of poetry. A literal translation loses its meaning and eloquence. Consequently, translators must also become editors if the spirit and meaning of translated works are to be retained. Yet, one always feels compelled to stay as close as possible to the exact literal translation, making only those editorial changes necessary to enhance readability and accurate conveyance of ideas. We have made every effort to provide just such a translation, changing as little as possible but editing where necessary in order to enhance understanding.

There is every reason to believe that Pareto would have encouraged the development of an easily readable translation true to the spirit of the original work. Indeed, the work Pareto himself prepared for publication in English is lucid and almost eloquent by comparison with most of his works translated into English by others. It therefore seems unlikely that he would have approved of stilted semantics and confusing terminology which sacrifice meaning at the expense of literal exactness. We follow Pareto's example in presenting *The Transformation of Democracy* in the style we believe he would have preferred.

Two types of editorial change were frequently made. First, many long sentences were broken up into shorter sentences in order to correspond with conventional English usage. Second, nouns were often inserted in the place of Pareto's pronouns in order to enhance clarity.

A number of other editorial changes, less systematic in nature, have also been made. In every case, the object has been to enhance readability and full conveyance of the meaning and spirit of Pareto's monograph. It is our belief that this carefully edited translation will be more accurate and more useful than a strictly literal translation.

Unless otherwise indicated, all footnotes are from the original text. Parentheses are used where Pareto himself used parentheses. Brackets are used in order to distinguish between material Pareto was quoting and the editorial quips Pareto inserted when he was quoting others, as well as to distinguish any material added to Pareto's text by the editor.

Acknowledgments

Our first acknowledgment goes to Jonathan Turner, who provided Charles Powers with the initial encouragement to read Pareto's works in 1977. It was under his tutelage that Powers clarified and systematized Pareto's insights. Moreover, it was during this period that preparing an English translation of *The Transformation of Democracy* became one of Powers's intellectual goals. Further intellectual stimulation and encouragement have come from Randall Collins, John Stanley, Reza Maghroori, and Allen Grimshaw.

The quality of the translation that follows is due to collaborative effort. However, Girola bore primary responsibility for the initial translation, while Powers bore primary responsibility for editing. We were provided with some additional translating assistance by Ms. Shellie Tellier.

Editorial assistance was provided by Joan Takahashi Powers, John Stanley, Dalia Buzin, and Irving Louis Horowitz. Helpful comments were provided by Whitney Pope, Juergen Backhaus, and Thomas Gieryn. Peter Burke, Gregory Travis, and Robert Elwood have been helpful in facilitating preparation of the manuscript. Norma MacKay and Jordan Henderson also assisted. Text editing facilities were provided by the Institute of Social Research, Indiana University, under the direction of James Lincoln at the time this project was initiated, and subsequently under the direction of David Knoke.

Charles H. Powers
Renata Girola

Introduction:

The Life and Times of Vilfredo Pareto

Charles H. Powers

Economists, political scientists, and sociologists have been highly selective in their reading of Pareto. Lacking familiarity with the breadth of his work, they often seem oblivious to the real issues Pareto was trying to address at different stages of his career or to the overarching theory he was systematically constructing. This introduction focuses on Pareto's intellectual maturation and identifies his overall theory of society.[1]

Family Background

Pareto is a relatively common name in the northwestern Mediterranean. Paretos are found from Catalonia in Spain to Tuscany in Italy. Throughout the Middle Ages this was a comparatively affluent zone of petty commodity production. Agriculture was diversified and crafts and trade were highly developed. Vilfredo Pareto's ancestors were successful merchants and supporters of the commercial order which made them prosperous.

From the end of the fifteenth century onward, the French and Austro-Hungarians vied for control of Northern Italy, while Italian principalities attempted to maintain their autonomy or even extend their interests by playing off the two superpowers against one another. Piedmont, controlled by the House of Savoy with its capital in Genoa, was particularly successful. This period also held good fortune for the Pareto family, which resided in Genoa. In 1719, Giovanni Lorenzo Bartolomeo Pareto, a grandfather of Vilfredo Pareto's great-grandfather, was ennobled with the hereditary title of Marquis.

Piedmont became one of the strongest Italian states, and the House of Savoy waged a constant war against the encroachment of French military power. But Vilfredo Pareto's grandfather and his grandfather's brother were ardent supporters of republicanism and assisted the French incursion during the Napoleonic Period. The importance of the Pareto family is attested to by the posts which family members held during that period. Giovanni Benedetto

2 The Transformation of Democracy

Pareto (1768-1831) was Senator of the Republic of Genoa, a member of the Legislative Council by order of Napoleon, and later Mayor of Genoa (1828). Giovanni Agostino Pareto (1773-1829) was Minister of Finance in the Napoleonic Republic of Liguria (1800-1802) and was nominated gonfalonier (or standard bearer) by Napoleon (1805). The Marquis Agostino went on to represent the Republic of Genoa at the Conference of Vienna in 1815.

After defeat of the French in the Napoleonic Wars, the Austro-Hungarian Empire strengthened its position throughout northern Italy and assumed direct control over Lombardy and Venice, thus threatening the interests and autonomy of Genoa. At the same time, Giuseppe Mazzini, born in Genoa in 1805 and therefore a contemporary of Pareto's father Raffaele (who was born in Genoa in 1812), pressed for the establishment of an Italian republic. As part of his republican program, he planned and participated in insurrections against the House of Savoy.

Mazzini enjoyed widespread support, including that of Pareto's family. Pareto's uncle Ernesto (1819-1893), son of Luigi, was imprisoned for his support of Mazzini. Pareto is even said to have had an aunt, of Irish extraction, who hid Mazzini during a police search by sewing him into a mattress. When Mazzini was forced into exile in 1834, many of his supporters followed. Among them was the Marquis Raffaele Pareto. Raffaele, who was to become a well-known hydrological engineer, moved to Paris in 1836 when he was twenty-four.

Another of Pareto's uncles, Lorenzo (1800-1865), son of Giovanni Agostino, also engaged in clandestine political activity. In 1847, along with Giorgio Doria and Vincenzo Ricci, Lorenzo Pareto instigated the political agitation that forced King Charles Albert to grant constitutional reforms. In the years that followed, Lorenzo served as Member of Parliament, Foreign Minister, and President of the Chamber of Deputies. In the meantime, Raffaele, still in exile in France, married Marie Mattenier (1816-1889), who is thought to have been a Calvinist. Raffaele and Marie were to have one son and two daughters. Vilfredo Frederico Damaso Pareto was born July 15, 1848.[2]

Vilfredo Pareto's Early Life, 1848-58

Family background factors were to have a profound effect on Vilfredo Pareto's life. The titled son of a privileged mercantile family living in Paris, Pareto enjoyed all the advantages society had to offer. He was provided with a classical education and raised in a culturally refined bilingual household. As a result he acquired all of the interpersonal skills and cultural resources a nineteenth-century man needed to travel in high circles.

But Pareto was also the son of an exile and a member of a family that had a tradition of fighting against autocrats and autocratic rule. Pareto grew up finding it natural to pit himself against established power. The character of his family milieu and childhood socialization determined the trademarks by which his later writings would be identified: suspicion of elites and revulsion from political rhetoric. Pareto was not an apologist for the status quo.

The period preceding and immediately following Pareto's birth was a tumultuous time in Italy. Intermittent struggles raged between the Austro-Hungarian Empire and the House of Savoy. Camillo Benso, Earl of Cavour, was made Prime Minister of Piedmont in 1852 and dampened republican sentiment by convincing people that the monarchy offered the only realistic basis for effective opposition against foreign domination. Exiles were invited to return to Italy when Cavour initiated a liberalization program designed to co-opt additional support for national unification under the House of Savoy. Raffaele returned sometime before 1855 and was joined by his family in 1858. The family settled in Turin, which was a center for returning dissidents.

The Teenage Years, 1858-65

Pareto returned with his family to Italy in 1858 and continued his schooling. He received a classical education in the Cartesian philosophy of universal doubt, mathematics, languages, history, and literature. The Cartesian influence was critical because it left Pareto untethered by any single school of thought and free to borrow from different philosophical positions and intellectual traditions. This ability to borrow from diverse traditions would prove to be a defining characteristic of Pareto's work in later years.

The 1860s were particularly exciting times for young people engaged in their initial voyages of intellectual discovery. Scientific advancements of the preceding two centuries had established a tone of scholastic excellence, as well as optimism about prospects for further accumulation of knowledge. In the area of social discourse, philosophical debates raged among the affluent and well educated (like Pareto) over atomistic vs. organic models of social order, the reliability of empirical investigation of social events, societal evolution, the possibility of developing a value-free social science, and the possibility of laws governing systems of social organization.

The College Years, 1865-69

Pareto's college years were spent at the Polytechnic Institute of Turin, and they mark a particularly important period in his life. In fact, the past failure of social scientists to understand Pareto's theory of society may well result from their ignorance of this period. For Pareto's approach to social scientific analysis was ultimately dominated by the epistemological outlook he developed as an engineering student.

Pareto's epistemology is clearly stated in the opening pages of his baccalaureate dissertation completed in 1869, where he specifies the requirements for adequate theory construction.[3] Scientific advance requires the description of dynamic interdependence among the generic elements of a system. Pareto maintains that (1) change is inevitable, (2) there is no way to know exactly which of the infinite possible combinations of available units will bond, and (3) uncontrolled extraneous influences affect observed outcomes. In light of these facts, theory should (1) focus on the dynamics of change rather than end states, (2) consider aggregate phenomena rather than the behavior of individual units, (3) specify the principles that seem to underly the most widespread or general processes, and (4) ignore extraneous factors. The actions of any given person are (like the behavior of single atomic particles) difficult if not impossible to predict. However, aggregate patterns can be studied, and the dynamics that produce those patterns can be understood. The conception of science Pareto developed as an engineer was to become an integral part of his analysis of complex social phenomena.

Substantive content of the dissertation is also of some importance. The proclivity for equilibrium analysis so apparent in Pareto's later works can be traced to his days as a student, for his dissertation is an attempt to describe equilibria in solids in terms of shifting balance among countervailing forces of expansion and contraction. Mutual dependence among system components necessitates that change in one system property will result in the establishment of a new balance among the full range of countervailing forces that determine the character of the system. The concept of equilibrium does not imply that existing systems are good, or that the world is static. Quite the opposite. All equilibria undergo change because any alteration within the system results in adjustment throughout the system. For Pareto, equilibrium theory seeks to specify the dynamics of change.

An unspoken assumption of the equilibrium perspective is that our theoretical models can be made sufficiently complete to enable prediction of system outcomes. This was Pareto's goal. Later stages of Pareto's work can be viewed as a gradual process of clarifying concepts, isolating generic properties, and discovering principles that would enable him to apply an equilibrium perspective in the analysis of social systems. Pareto's social thought cannot be adequately understood without first grasping the vision of scientific explanation he had developed as a college student. He constructed social theory following the physical sciences as his model.

Pareto as an Engineer, 1869-89

Vilfredo Pareto's first job (1869-74) was as a consulting engineer for the Rome Railway Company. Although accounts of this period differ, he seems to have been transferred from Rome to Florence in 1872.

An engineer by profession, Pareto's hobby was the study of political economy. In the years following Italian unification in 1871, the excitement of addressing complex national problems, setting national policy, and charting a course for national development drew many learned people into the political arena. Pareto was among them. He gained local acclaim and the respect of the influential Peruzzi family, for a lecture titled "Proportional Representation" presented to the Academy of Geography in Florence on June 29, 1872. This lecture, which was published later that year by the Academy's newsletter, makes it clear that Pareto adopted many of the political sentiments of his family.

Another turning point occurred in 1874 when Pareto accepted a post as the superintendent of Societá Ferriere Italiana, an iron foundry in the Valley of the Arno with headquarters in Florence (1874-89). His interest in political economy was stimulated on a number of corporate business trips to England and Scotland. An enthusiastic Pareto began to frequent the Adam Smith Society, which met at the house of the renowned hostess Emilia Toscanelli-Peruzzi. There he made the acquaintance of the best minds of Florence. An indication of the changes Pareto was experiencing was that at this time he mastered Greek and Latin. Besides translating classics for literary purposes, Pareto read original texts in his attempt to account for the rise and decline of great civilizations.

During this period Pareto became an outspoken advocate of free trade. This position put Pareto at odds with economic and political elites who were using government as a tool to further personal interests. Yet these elites claimed to be concerned only with the national welfare. It was then that Pareto developed an unshakable belief that rulers devise misleading rhetoric in order to cloak the greedy nature of their own activities.

Pareto acquired a following and, at the age of 33, decided to run for Parliament from the district of Peruzzi on a free-trade platform. In point of fact, he was an anti-elitist radical, and his unsuccessful candidacy produced bitter disappointment. He reached the conclusion that people hear only what they want to hear and ignore the truth. Arriving at this conclusion marked another important juncture in Pareto's development as a social scientist.

Pareto became somewhat more retiring after the death of his father late in 1882. He continued in his position as superintendent at the foundry, while periodically contributing articles on political economy for newspapers and magazines.

Pareto as a Commentator, 1889-92

In 1889 Pareto married a Russian woman named Dina Bakunin, resigned his engineering position, and moved with his wife and mother to Villa Rosa in Frisole. He was then forty-one years of age and able to live rather comfortably on consulting fees. Pareto began a career as a commentator, apparently with the long-range goal of obtaining a university teaching position. He published over 160 articles during this brief period and authorities came to regard him as a rather dangerous person. Italian police are said to have disbanded a number of his speaking engagements.

Most of the articles Pareto wrote during this period are polemic.[4] He was a strict advocate of free trade, open competition, and freedom from government intervention, and his commentaries were designed to convince people that laissez-faire policies promote general prosperity. He argued that governments err by passing tariffs, granting monopoly rights to large corporations, erecting barriers against the entry of new firms into markets, providing government subsidies and loans, instituting make-work programs, and supporting high wages for workers. Pareto was a vocal opponent of militarism and colonial expansion, which he regarded as immoral and as diversions of funds from meaningful capital investment. Although he began to champion the rights of the working class, before another decade would pass he came to perceive the same self-serving greed and hypocrisy among the workers that he recognized in the wealthy.

Pareto was perplexed that political systems benefiting a few at the expense of many can continue to exist. He determined that corrupt structures successfully resist change because zeal for reform quickly erodes among those who profit, even in small ways, from the system. Most people support the status quo for the sole reason that organizations co-opt support by dispensing rewards. Overt repression of dissidents is seldom necessary because people preoccupy themselves by trying to make small personal gains rather than participating in revolt. And any real threat of disorder can be dispelled by the speedy, judicious, strategic use of force.

Having been trained as an engineer, Pareto understood what the goals and methods of a science should be. But social science was not securely established in the 1880s. Understandably, his early articles on political economy took the form of journalistic commentary rather than social science. Nonetheless, writing commentary provided Pareto with an opportunity to sharpen his sociological insights. In the absence of any well-developed social theory, Pareto had to isolate the important features of social phenomena for himself. He focused on cyclical socioeconomic and political change.

Just as Pareto had developed an epistemological outlook in his earlier stage as an engineering student, the substantive ingredients for a theory of society were uncovered by him as he wrote journalistic commentary. Yet the task of generating real hypotheses and integrating these hypotheses into a sophisticated theory of social systems remained unfinished.

Pareto as an Economist, 1892-98

By the time Pareto was forty-four, his work was attracting considerable attention among economists. Pareto's admission to the inner circles of economic scholarship was based largely on his response (in 1891) to Maffeo Pantaleoni's *Pure Economics* (1889). Pantaleoni's work convinced Pareto that social science was possible and that economics would be the first social field to develop into a real science. The tangible nature of economic concepts appealed to Pareto's engineering orientation. Inspired by Pantaleoni's work, Pareto wrote a series of articles that excited intellectuals of the period. Pantaleoni and Pareto developed a lifelong friendship and correspondence. Encouraged by Pantaleoni, Pareto began an effort to formalize Leon Walras's equilibrium models of the economy, much as he had formalized the equilibrium theory of solids in his dissertation. It was on the strength of this work, and that of Pantaleoni's recommendation, that Pareto was invited to assume a position at the University of Lausanne in 1892.[5] His primary attention immediately turned from commentary to the establishment of mathematical economics as a substantive area of inquiry. He apparently enjoyed this change to more academic pursuits and was successful in establishing a school of thought.

Pareto published *Course in Political Economy* in 1896-97.[6] This work, which developed as Pareto assumed responsibility for teaching what had been Walras's old course in political economy, firmly established Pareto as one of the major economists of his time. It is a description of the interrelated nature of economic phenomena. In it, Pareto utilizes marginal utility and supply and demand functions in order to formalize equilibrium models of economic behavior. At the time it was published, this book marked a significant advance in economic thinking. Economists continue to be informed by the concept of optimality Pareto employed in that analysis (although he would not necessarily approve of the way the concept is currently employed).

It was also in *Course in Political Economy* that Pareto introduced his law of income distribution, more fully developed in a later series of articles. He contended that wealth is distributed with a constant income differential between the "haves" and the "have nots" in any society. Sociopolitical changes are unlikely to produce permanent reductions in inequality, because those in control of social institutions will always try to profit at the expense of others. Therefore, people cannot seriously anticipate the elimination of inequality. But poverty can be reduced by increasing productivity. Put more colloquially, if the pie is always going to be sliced unevenly, then the best way to help the poor is by enlarging the pie.

An event occurred at the height of Pareto's renown as an economist that was to substantially affect him the remainder of his life. One of Pareto's uncles died in 1898, leaving him a small fortune valued at well over $1 million in 1984 prices. This inheritance would enable Pareto to move to the country and lead a quiet life, free from worry or distraction and devoted to his writing.

Pareto as a Political Economist and Political Sociologist, 1898-1906

Pareto challenged the narrow position that economic events can or should be studied in isolation. Instead, Pareto maintained that economic phenomena can only be adequately understood within the sociopolitical contexts in which they occur. He must have had many long and involved conversations on this subject, for between 1898 and 1901 Pareto harbored a number of political refugees wanted by the Italian police.

In 1898 Pareto began to teach sociology in addition to economics. This teaching assignment provided him with an opportunity to more systematically explore the connections among social, economic, and political phenomena. The direction of Pareto's work is best reflected in his "An Application of Sociological Theory" (1901), which outlines an elaborate, systematic, and powerful theory of social systems.[7] Pareto sought to identify the major features of society that fluctuate cyclically, to describe the movement of these cycles in equilibrium terms, and to indicate ways in which the structural features of society emerge from the equilibria being described.

The most striking feature of this work is an initial statement of the theory of circulation of elites for which Pareto has become so well known. "Lions" with strong will and forthright manner rule by force. They lose power to "foxes" who are more devious and rule through cunning and deceit. In turn, rule by "foxes" gives way to rule by "lions," and so on in cyclical fashion.

What is frequently forgotten is that Pareto intended his description of the circulation of elites to be a single aspect of his more encompassing theory of society, and to serve as a model to be used in specifying other aspects of this encompassing theory. "An Application of Sociological Theory" is predicated upon the position that people are deeply motivated by *sentiments*, or subconscious beliefs that serve as standards of evaluation. Although Pareto eventually identified six categories of sentiments, two are of primary importance. These are "combination" and "group persistence." "Combination" refers to craft and cunning. This sentiment is sometimes misinterpreted as desire to experiment or innovate, but deceitful craft and cunning are clearly implied in the Italian meaning of the term *combinazioni*. "Group persistence" is the tendency to resist change and stubbornly adhere to established ways. Individuals are characterized by a mixture of both sentiments, but every individual tends to be dominated by one or the other. The distribution of these sentiments varies within any population over time. Aggregate patterns of popular sentiments are important because they set parameters on the types of behavior to be tolerated and encouraged within a given society.

Aggregate sentiments among elites are also important. Pareto maintained in 1901 that at any given point in time political elites are composed of some combination of "lions" and "foxes." "Lions," among whom sentiments of group persistence are strong, tend to be strong-willed, direct, conservative persons who favor adherence to tradition. "Foxes," among whom sentiments of combination are particularly strong, tend to be cunning, devious, and diplomatic. "Lions" prefer to exercise control by relying heavily on force to gain compliance and to operate through centralized mechanisms. "Foxes," on the other hand, prefer decentralized control based on co-optation and ideological manipulation as strategies for rule. (Pareto was later to modify his analysis and forego crude psychologism in favor of a more structural analysis.)

Pareto thought that economic elites circulate in the same way. "Rentiers," or members of the economic elite in whom sentiments of group persistence are strong, tend to act in ways which promote long-term rather than short-term economic growth by investing resources in basic industries. On the other hand, "speculators," who are strong in sentiments of combination, act in ways that maximize short-term economic growth but reduce the potential of long-term growth by investing resources in activities that may be profitable but comparatively unproductive.

Pareto culminates his analysis with discussion of the interrelated nature of political, economic, and social cycles. For instance, changes in public sentiment directly influence aggregate levels of saving in society, and consequently influence the amount of capital available for investment. By illustrating the reasons why social, economic, and political change are inherently cyclical and intrinsically interrelated, Pareto presents his first unified theory of society as a totality.

Pareto's social life deteriorated as his emerging theory began to take shape. His radical friends took issue with the position that they were self-serving ideologues. It was at this point (1901) that Pareto's wife seems to have absconded with household valuables and run away with a socialist. Jane Régis (born 1877) entered his life shortly thereafter and remained his lifelong companion and love.

Pareto was able to balance his interests in economics, sociology, and political science throughout this period. Among his more sociological works was an important statement on ideology (1902-03), in which he argued that behavior is motivated by non-logical considerations, which are covered in a veneer of ex post facto pseudological rationalization.[8] Pareto was also making economic breakthroughs. In 1906 he published *Manual of Political Economy*, which advances significantly beyond *Course in Political Economy*
. Pareto resigned his chair and moved into semi-retirement in 1907. He continued to teach courses at Lausanne, although with decreasing frequency. But far from becoming less active, Pareto took advantage of this last opportunity to make a final burst of contributions to the social sciences. In 1909 he published a revised edition of *Manual of Political Economy*, which has long been regarded as a classic in economics.[9] He proceeded, satisfied with his economic contributions, to what he believed would be the most important contribution of his career.

Pareto as a Sociologist, 1907-14

While completing the second edition of his *Manual of Political Economy*, Pareto began what he expected to be his greatest work. He actually began his *Treatise on General Sociology* in 1907.[10] It was to occupy all of his time from 1909 until its completion in 1914. Norberto Bobbio captures Pareto's mood at the time.[11]

Pareto, having given up lecturing, immured at home with his cats, was deaf to any other call but that of driving ahead with his *Treatise* which assumed terrifying proportions in his hands. It is an intense, exclusive and absorbing work, written in a state of continual excitement and amidst great hopes, as if he were a gold prospector.

Pareto resided with Madame Régis in a comfortable villa affectionately referred to as Casa Angora because of Pareto's penchant for his eighteen Angora cats. Casa Angora was located in one of the world's most beautiful villages. Céligny overlooks Lake Geneva between the cities of Geneva and Lausanne. This is an agricultural area of gently rolling hills covered with rich grass. This tranquil community of helpful people, cool water, invigorating air, and magnificent pastoral scenery can put a restless soul at ease. Pareto maintained a parklike garden in which to write, relax, and occasionally indulge his tastes for fine wine and fresh fruit.

Nonetheless, this was a painful time for Pareto. Most of his old students and colleagues were unsympathetic to Pareto's newly found interest in sociology. They regarded as ludicrous blasphemy the position that economic cycles are determined by the social and political forces which economists typically ignore. Pareto retreated with Madame Régis and his cats to the picturesque country village he had made his home, living out the remainder of his life in relative isolation while maintaining active correspondence with a few intimates such as Maffeo Pantaleoni and Georges Sorel. These were the circumstances that earned Pareto his title as "the lone thinker of Céligny."

Pareto regarded *Treatise on General Sociology* as his most important work. Unfortunately, this one-million-word tome is also his most misunderstood work. Awkward terms like "residue" and "derivation" have created unnecessary confusion. "Residues" are observable behaviors, and "derivations" are delusions or stories people invent in order to justify their actions. Pareto treated "residues" and "derivations" as empirical indicators of people's

Table 1: Demystifying Important Terms

1. Sentiments — Deep-seated values or evaluative standards.
   - 1a. Combination — A type of sentiment. Combination is a direct translation of the Italian term "combinazioni" meaning deceit, craft, cunning, and guile. Pareto identified any era when sentiments of combination are strong as a period of "skepticism."
   - 1b. Group Persistence — A type of sentiment. Group persistence implies stubborn adherence to established ways. Pareto identified any era when sentiments of group persistence are strong as a period of "faith."
2. Residues — Behavioral manifestations reflecting the sentiments people hold.
3. Derivations — Verbal manifestations reflecting the sentiments people hold. Stories and delusions people fabricate in order to rationalize actions.

"sentiments," or subconscious value orientations that serve as standards of evaluation. Although they sound awkward and unfamiliar at first glance, Pareto's terms actually have clear and straightforward meanings with intuitive appeal. Earlier translators may have done Pareto a disservice by adhering to literal translations (e.g. "residue," "combination," and "group persistence") rather than conveying Pareto's intended meaning as fully and accurately as possible.

The most disastrous error readers can make is to think Pareto develops a theory of "residues" and "derivations." Instead, Pareto employs residues and derivations as empirical indicators of other things. Pareto's work is like that of modern-day researchers who construct empirical indicators to measure abstract properties.

In much the same way that Comte saw sociology as the queen science, so Pareto envisioned his *Treatise on General Sociology* as an encompassing social scientific theory for understanding and forecasting cycles in business, politics, and public sentiment. As emphasized earlier, Pareto did not believe it would be possible to understand patterns of economic change outside of the sociopolitical contexts in which those changes occur. This is why he surrendered the prestige he received as an economist in favor of pursuing a fledgling field of study. Sociological theory held more promise, in his estimation, than did mainstream economics. This follows, in part, from the fact that Pareto sought to account for the features of social organization which economists generally treat as givens.

Treatise on General Sociology prepares the groundwork for analysis of society as a complex system of interrelated parts in equilibrium. It is in this tome that the concept of social system is most forcefully employed, with social, economic, and political variables bound to one another in relationships of mutual determination. A change in any aspect of the social system necessitates changes in the rest of the system. Changes in the character of social systems must therefore be understood in terms of mutual dependence among system elements. It was from Pareto that Talcott Parsons would later borrow the concept of system and introduce it as a dominant metaphor in sociology.[12]

Pareto began his sociological work by attempting to justify the existence of sociology as a discipline. He proceeded by devoting the first three volumes of *Treatise on General Sociology* to a laborious defense of assumptions which, in his view, necessitated the development of sociology as a new field of inquiry. First, human behavior is, for the most part, non-logical. Therefore, it cannot be understood within the context of traditional economic models. Second, human behavior is motivated by sentiments. Sentiments change rhythmically over time, so that adherence to tradition ("faith") is encouraged during certain periods, and receptivity to change ("skepticism") is strong during other periods. Hence, patterns of human behavior cannot be viewed as either constant or as historically unique. And third, human behavior is not motivated by the forces to which people attribute their actions. Ideology and conventional wisdom are, therefore, inadequate explanations for behavior. In large part, then, the first three volumes of the *Treatise on General Sociology* highlight the errors to be found in previous explanations of social phenomena. It is in this way that these first three volumes set the stage for the systematic development of Pareto's theory to be found in the fourth volume.

Pareto viewed the first three volumes of *Treatise* as an effort to justify and lay the preliminary groundwork for a scientific study of society. By 1913 when Pareto began work on the fourth volume he was 65 years old, and readers sense that he felt some remorse for having spent so much time on preliminaries while leaving himself little time for elaborating his own formal theory of social organization. Pareto began volume 4 with a clear mission. He intended to use a few fundamental principles to explain and predict patterns of socioeconomic and political change. Wishing to explore many issues, Pareto sought to save time by employing familiar examples. As a result, volume 4 sometimes seems like an elaboration of "An Application of Sociological Theory."

Economic activity diversifies during prosperous times. Diversification is, at first, to the advantage of average citizens. But inequities increase as speculators and occupational parasites invent ways of acquiring high incomes without being productive. In other words, economic activity is not synonymous with productive activity. Speculation is contagious, and nations periodically enter periods when people are less interested in building a future with their own hard work than they are in trying to devise ways of getting something for nothing by reaping fruits from the labor of others.

During prosperous periods, economic activity comes to be concentrated in consumer-oriented industries. Need for capital increases with economic expansion per se, and as consumer-oriented industries grow because these businesses have high rates of capital depletion. At the same time, the availability of physical capital declines because of disproportionate investment of energy in activities that are non-capital producing. Economic contraction begins as the need for physical capital outstrips the capacity of the economy to generate those goods, and as more and more people come to make their livings by inhibiting rather than facilitating the productive activities of others.

As contraction sets in, the consumer-oriented sectors of the economy experience severe dislocation. Demand for capital declines during initial stages of economic contraction because few people have the confidence to invest in new enterprise and because the infrastructure shrinks in size. As the downturn worsens, demand for physical capital falls below capital production and excess physical capital accumulates. Frustration with the inhibiting practices of lawyers and bureaucrats also builds and a reaction sets in. Accumulation of physical capital then encourages investment in basic industries and economic expansion. Hence, oscillation between periods of economic expansion and contraction is, in Pareto's view, inevitable.

Future economic trends can be predicted by monitoring changes in the variables Pareto identified. His analysis of these system dynamics can be readily translated into a series of propositions.

Table 2: The Dynamics of Productivity

1. The greater the availability of physical capital and willingness to invest (6), then the more probable that an increase in productivity becomes.
2. The greater the increase in productivity (1), then the greater the expansion of the consumer sector of the economy relative to the capital-producing sector.
3. The larger the economy and the lower the relative commitment of resources to the capital-producting sector (2), then (a) the more serious that capital shortages will be and (b) the more hesitant people will be to invest in the expansion of basic industries.
4. The more serious that capital shortages become and the more hesitant people are to invest in expansion of basic industries (3), then the more probable that economic contraction becomes.
5. The more productivity declines (4), then (a) the greater the decline of the consumer sector relative to the capital-producing sector.
6. The smaller the economy and the greater the relative commitment of resources in capital-producing industries (5), then the greater the availability of usable capital (in excess of replacement needs) and the less hesitant people will be to invest in the expansion of basic industries.

Table 2 and the other tables to follow attempt to capture and summarize Pareto's theoretical insights. Once Pareto's ideas are clearly and succinctly communicated, readers will be free to assess them and to borrow selectively.

Cyclical change in the political sphere occurs in the same undulatory fashion as the business cycle. Rule by the "fox" tends to be characterized by patronage, co-optation, and control via large, complex, decentralized political machines. Rule by "lions" tends to be characterized by use of force, centralized control, and small bureaucracies with clear lines of hierarchical authority. The form of society changes with pendulous movement on this political cycle. Exclusive reliance on force and centralized control generates widespread opposition. Because the use of force can only be effective if there is adequate surveillance, social control breaks down when resistance grows and overtaxes the capacity of control agencies to monitor the activities of potential insurgents. Under such circumstances, government functionaries must begin to rely upon decentralized control and co-optation as means of gaining compliance. But new control problems inhere in maintaining control through patronage and co-optation. Put simply, decentralized administration places great reliance on unsupervised activity, and too many people are allowed to engage in activities which inhibit the productivity of others. Employing patronage to gain compliance also requires enormous expenditure of funds. Moreover, decentralized systems seem incapable of employing force when its expeditious use is required to quell political opposition. Thus, overreliance on either organizational strategy results in integrative problems and eventually leads to undulating structural change. This more structural analysis is quite illuminating and makes considerable progress in overcoming the problems found in Pareto's early (1901) articulation of the psychologistic (e.g. "lions" vs. "foxes") version of the theory.

Table 3: The Dynamics of Political Change

7. The greater the erosion of central authority (12), then the greater the use of co-optation as a means of social control.
8. When central authority is eroded, the more co-optation is relied upon as a means of social control (7), then the more problematic social control becomes, in part because too many people are allowed to engage in self-interested activities which inhibit the productivity of others.
9. When central authority is eroded, the more problematic social control becomes (8), then the more pressure builds for consolidation of central authority.
10. The greater the consolidation of central authority (9), then the greater the use of force as a means of social control.
11. When central authority is consolidated, the more force is relied upon as an instrument of social control (10), then the more problematic social control becomes, in part because the arbitrary use of force generates resentment.
12. When central authority is consolidated, the more problematic social control becomes (11), then the more pressure for decentralization builds.

Changes in public sentiment lag slightly behind changes in the economic and political domains as aggregate shifts occur between periods of faith and periods of skepticism. Periods of faith are characterized by stubborn adherence to established ways, traditionalism, and propensity to save. Periods of skepticism, on the other hand, are characterized by widespread deceit, a relaxed attitude toward craft, pseudological ideologies, economic speculation, propensity to spend rather than save, and sexual permissiveness.

Undulation between faith and skepticism is inevitable because of man's unending quest for a belief system which is both useful and realistic. First one and then the other receives disproportionate emphasis in public sentiment as people attempt to find an acceptable balance between the two. During periods in which skepticism reigns, people are left without clear prescriptions for behavior. Reacting against normlessness, public sentiment comes to favor the development of relatively clear and inflexible normative guidelines. But while firm rules initially provide people with a sense of comfort, the inflexible application of norms eventually generates tension. Another reaction occurs and people become more receptive to change. The cycle thus renews itself.

Once again, Pareto suggests a series of principles that enable observers to monitor and forecast social change. In this instance, change in popular beliefs is forecast.

Table 4: Change in Popular Sentiments

13. The more equivocal norms become (18), then the less constrained people are in their actions, the freer people are to pursue immediate gratification, and the more likely non-productive and counterproductive activities are to be tolerated.
14. The less constrained people are in their actions (13), then the more conflict there will be over definitions of appropriate behavior.
15. The greater the level of conflict over definitions of appropriate behavior (14), then the more likely people are to seek coherent traditions and unequivocal prescriptions.
16. The less equivocal prescriptions become (15), then the more constrained people are, the more inclined people are to forego immediate gratification, and the less likely non-productive and counterproductive activities are to be tolerated.
17. The more constrained people are in their actions (16), then the more likely they are to question the rationality of normative beliefs.
18. The more people question the rationality of normative beliefs (17), then the more likely they are to seek relaxed prescriptions.

As noted above, an important component in Pareto's analysis is that economic, political, and belief cycles tend to synchronize one another, with the belief cycle lagging slightly. Thus, Pareto presents us with an image of rhythmic socioeconomic and political change.

The cycles synchronize one another in a variety of ways. For instance, propensity to save is greater during periods of faith than during periods of skepticism, and propensity to save directly effects the availability of capital for investment and economic expansion.[13] Relaxation of norms and erosion of central authority in the face of special interests foster accelerated speculation and transformation of the economic infrastructure. Conversely, economic growth and diversification initially stimulate (in a feedback process) still greater desire for relaxed behavioral prescriptions and more pressing needs for decentralization of political control. Economic contraction, on the other hand, creates different life experiences and administrative needs, promoting conservatism and centralization of political control. Conservatism and con-

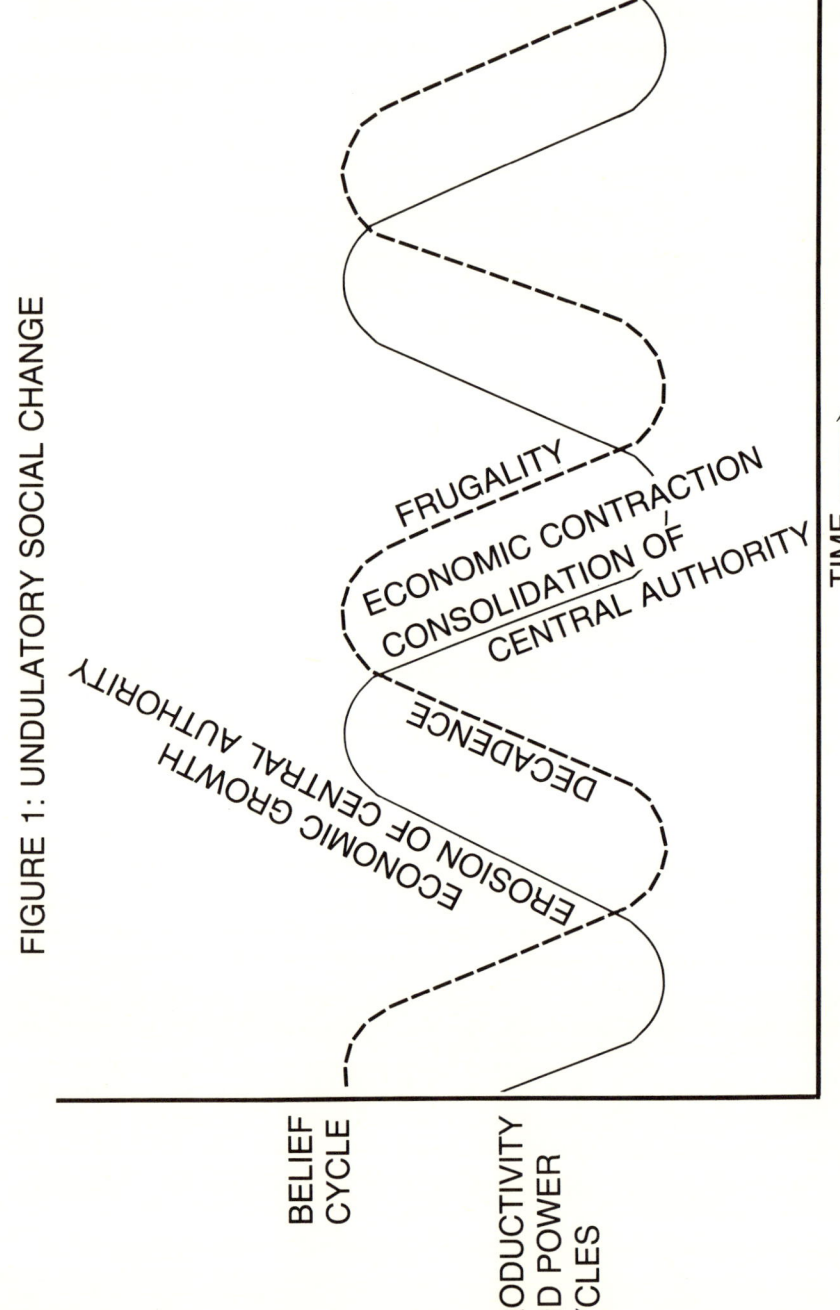

solidation of central power act to impede speculation. These changes work together to produce socioeconomic and political transformation. While others satisfy themselves with the assertion that things oscillate, Pareto strives to discover the dynamics that make cyclical change an inherent and unavoidable feature of social life. What emerges from his *Treatise on General Sociology* is an illuminating set of testable principles, which provide a forceful and compelling view of human history.

The Ultimate Disappointment, 1915-19

Wartime exigencies prevented the publication of Pareto's *Treatise on General Sociology* until 1916. Once it was published Pareto was clearly disappointed by the reception it received. Many readers were rather bored by the first three volumes. Even more unfortunate, most readers became mired in empirical detail and completely lost sight of the general theory of society Pareto was attempting to construct. Few seem to have been aware that Pareto was identifying the dynamics that give rise to cyclical change in the economy, the polity, and in public sentiment.

Instead of recognizing Pareto's intent and properly identifying what Pareto regarded as his real contribution, most readers viewed his *Treatise on General Sociology* as little more than a compendium of awkward terms. Such a complete misreading was a source of great pain and anguish in Pareto's last years. He was aging and suffered from heart disease, which forced him to limit his activities and isolate himself. Readers failed to comprehend what he was trying to say. Pareto began to doubt whether people were capable of appreciating a theory that attempted to provide a scientific account of complex social phenomena. His sense of disillusionment was deep. But he did what he could to leave readers with a more accurate vision of his emerging theory by writing letters, publishing commentaries, and responding to reviews.

At the same time, events in Italy and the rest of the world were confirming Pareto's predictions. Common people began to view World War I as an adventure that benefited the rich at the expense of the working class. Consumerism and the desire for easy living spread. Twenty-two million work days were lost to strike activity in Italy during 1919 alone, and the November elections demonstrated the depth of popular support for the Socialist Party. Meanwhile, the national government was incapacitated by indecision. The upper class vacillated between a desire to appease workers and a reactionary fear of social revolution. Violent clashes were on the increase and fear thrived. It was in this milieu that Italian fascism took root. Pareto wrote his final series of articles in this context.

Pareto's Final Statement, 1920-21

Pareto's work was often misunderstood by critics and supporters alike. He made a final effort to capsulize and clarify his theory of society in a collection of essays published serially in *Rivista di Milano* in 1920, and then published together as *The Transformation of Democracy* in 1921.[14]

The first of the serialized articles to appear in *The Transformation of Democracy* was "Generalizations," published on May 5, 1920. If "Generalizations" seems choppy it is for good reason. This brief paper is Pareto's own personal summary of the insights he regarded as most important from the first three volumes of *Treatise on General Sociology*. As such, "Generalizations" is an exceedingly important article, for it resolves much of the confusion surrounding Pareto's most voluminous and convoluted work. Pareto reviews a number of issues. The first is that cyclical change is inexorable. People who believe in utopian ideologies may think that conditions can continue to improve forever, but they are filled with false hope.

Cyclical movement is inexorable largely because people perceive and respond to events in terms of sentiments, or deep-seated evaluative standards. Their aggregate pattern of response to unfolding events is therefore predictable and can create the conditions for further social change including oscillatory reaction. For example, Pareto characterized Italian society in 1920 as strong in the sentiments of combinations. On aggregate, people had come to feel that they should grow prosperous without having to work hard. As a consequence more energy was invested in connivance and in devising ways of transferring existing wealth than in constructive activity and the production of new wealth. With workers engaged in prolonged strikes and capitalists busy with parasitic or speculative activities yielding quick and easy money, no class was contributing to sustained growth or real prosperity.

Important trends being observed by Pareto included (1) the erosion of central authority, (2) the transformation of democracy into a plutocracy in which vested interests use the government as a tool for their own profit, and (3) the mutation and spread of counterproductive sentiments as people are changed by the smell of easy money. These three trends were the subjects of the next three articles in the series.

Chapter 2, "The Crumbling of Central Authority," was published in two segments on May 20 and June 5 of 1920. This chapter deals with cyclical change in administrative agencies. Countervailing forces of centralization and decentralization of power operate to produce wavelike oscillation in the structure of coordination and control in a society. Periods of political centralization are followed by periods of political decentralization, and back again. In Pareto's view, the 1920s were to be a period of dangerous erosion in the authority of central governments.

A central government has authority only when it has the power and the will to adjudicate grievances and dispense justice throughout its realm. When subjects cannot look to the central government for protection, it loses legitimacy.

The postwar era seemed to Pareto to be a period in which people openly flaunted their ability to defy the law. Bureaucrats actually contributed to the decline of governmental power and legitimacy by tolerating or even condoning blatant disrespect for institutionalized authority. The government seemed completely impotent in the face of organized interest groups. Corporate giants and organized labor were granted whatever concessions they asked for, at the expense of the general public.

When the Italian government proved unable to enforce even minor decisions such as the implementation of daylight savings time in offices of the government-owned railway, Pareto had to ask if the government was capable of making and enforcing any decisions at all. Over what realms of activity could the government exert its sovereignty? Pareto's answer was that the authority of the central government was crumbling away. He regarded this as an important step in the transformation of democracy, for if the government is incapable of resisting the unreasonable or illicit demands of some, it is equally incapable of protecting the rights of others.

Chapter 3, "The Plutocratic Cycle," was published on July 5, 1920. This chapter fits Pareto's insights on the erosion of authority in Italy into a broader historical context. Democratic governments fall unsuspecting prey to the baser instinct of greed. Special interests trade favor for favor, and democratic rule for the common good is transformed into plutocratic rule by the few for the good of the few. Of course, plutocrats try to maintain the facade of democracy in order to delude the gullible masses.

True representative government invariably gives way to plutocracy, or government by the wealthy. Plutocracy can assume two different forms, both of which have long-term destabilizing effects. "Military" plutocracies rely on the use of force to maintain social control. But widespread use of force by government agencies spawns resistance. As resistance grows, pressure for democratization increases, and those in control lose power. Democracy fades as a new breed of wealthy people, claiming to represent the interests of the masses, take control. The new plutocratic elite maintains itself by granting concessions in order to co-opt support for their rule. This was the stage in which Italy found itself at the time Pareto was writing. "Demagogic" plutocracy is the most insidious form of government for two reasons. First, those who rule by covertly purchasing support are generally more concerned with devising ways to divert existing wealth than in exploring avenues for the creation of new wealth. Hence, their rule ultimately undermines national prosperity. Second, such rulers tend to be devious and cunning, and can therefore stay in power for long periods by manipulating the sentiments of the masses. Their power is maintained until they bankrupt the government, disrupt the economy, and offend the conservative inclinations of common people. Once the inner contradictions of rule through co-optation become clear, cyclical movement in the opposite direction is initiated, and "military" plutocracy emerges. Thus, Pareto seems to forecast the rise of Italian fascism in the 1920s.

The real value of this essay, along with the others, is that Pareto eludes to the pitfalls which subvert the fragile character of democratic government. His analysis suggests that cyclical dynamics can be observed in any nation, without regard to geographic location or time. He is, therefore, alerting us to our future as well as detailing the past.

Chapter 4, "Sentiments," was published on July 20, 1920. In it, Pareto noted that speculation was ruining the industrial world. Sadly, Pareto expected this trend to become more pronounced before it would show any signs of easing. Put simply, sentiments had been transformed to such a degree that even common people began to respond to situations with cunning deceit rather than hard work, and with larceny rather than honest intentions in their hearts. People came to believe that they should be able to grow prosperous through no effort of their own. Such orientations undermine rather than promote national prosperity. The spread of combinazioni, of deceitful cunning and wile, could only mean that plutocratic tendencies would increase and that economic strength would be further sapped. This was to continue until irreversible contradictions emerged, heralding a crisis of devastating proportions.

Late in 1920, "Generalizations," "The Crumbling of Central Authority," "The Plutocratic Cycle," and "Sentiments" were being prepared for publication as a monograph. In October Pareto wrote an "Appendix" to accompany the earlier chapters.[15] The purpose of this appendix was to take stock and assess what he had said in the earlier chapters. His assessment was that a catastrophe was approaching at an even more rapid pace that he had earlier envisioned. The rise of fascism and the Great Depression confirm the accuracy of his predictions.

The Transformation of Democracy appeared in Italian in 1921. It is of major importance precisely because Pareto felt his earlier work had been so thoroughly misunderstood. Hence, for Pareto, *The Transformation of Democracy* was a final effort to emphasize what he regarded as the most important elements of his theory. Pareto was interested in cyclical change produced by a shifting balance among countervailing forces of centralization and decentralization of power, expansion and contraction in forces of economic production, and "faith" versus "skepticism" in public sentiment. By what it omits, *The Transformation of Democracy* demonstrates that purely psychologistic interpretations of Pareto's work are in error. The task of observant readers is to be informed by the lessons Pareto teaches.

It is instructive to note that Pareto had come to view himself as the unrecognized Albert Einstein of the social sciences. He introduced the concept of relativity into sociology and developed theoretical principles capturing the implications of relativity for societal phenomena. That he saw himself in this light seems clear from the letter he wrote to Pantaleoni on May 22, 1921:

> My *Treatise on Sociology* is an attempt, however imperfect, to introduce into the social sciences that *relativity* which, in a much more perfect way, has now been introduced into the physical sciences. From the metaphysical absolute, we are gradually moving towards experimental reality. A tremendous step forward had been made by Galileo, Copernicus, and Newton. Another is now being made by Einstein. Who knows whether, a century from now, an odd copy of *Sociology* will have escaped being devoured by the rats, and some researcher will find that, at the beginning of the twentieth century, there was an author who tried to introduce the principle of relativity into the social sciences. And he will say: "Why on earth was this not understood, when this principle made such easy inroads into the physical sciences?" I think he will reply: "Because at that time, as at all times, the social sciences were immensely backward as compared with the physical sciences."[16]

In Einstein's work, relativity implies that measurement of speed and distance depend upon the vantage point of the observer. (This is entirely different from saying that several measurements taken from the same place will be erratic.) In Pareto's view, the interpretations and responses individuals have to events in the social world are also determined by vantage point. Conservatives and liberals, for example, see the world through different sets of rose-colored glasses. Where they "sit" determines what they see and how they respond.

For Einstein, all people on one planet stand in the same place in relationship to the rest of the universe. Therefore, all those people see the universe moving by in the same way. For Pareto, people sharing the same sentiments will have similar assessments of events in the social world. Since the citizens of a given society are influenced by the aggregate pattern of prevailing sentiments, their aggregate pattern of responses to events can be predicted. Such response patterns have major consequences for cyclical change. For example, mass optimism affects levels of consumption and saving, both of which have impact on the business cycle. The path is paved for expansion of the consumer sector when there seems to be an aggregate proclivity for conspicuous consumption. Similarly, faith and frugality encourage respect for central authority and the accumulation of a large pool of public savings available for investment. Thus aggregate patterns of sentiment can foster basic transformations in economic infrastructure and systems of government. It is in this way that Pareto's "theory of relativity" gains real interest for students of economics, politics, and general social change.

Pareto's Last Years, 1922-23

Pareto was a disaffected liberal. He had complete confidence in himself and was thoroughly irreligious. But by 1922 heart disease was causing very serious health problems. Although he maintained written correspondence with a few trusted friends and associates, he rarely escaped the confines of his country home. A divorce was finally secured from his first wife early in 1923, enabling Pareto and Madame Régis to marry.

Shortly before his death, Pareto was accorded recognition from Mussolini.[17] For this reason, combined with his denouncements of hypocrisy on the part of leftists, he was labelled a fascist by many intellectuals. But this label was neither charitable nor informed. Pareto opposed plutocracy throughout his life. Above all, Pareto's real conscience is to be found in his constant opposition to military adventurism, such as the war with Turkey over Libya in 1911 and, of course, his opposition to World War I. Pareto's biggest mistake seems to have been his even-handedness. Willing to denounce hypocrisy and greed on the part of all parties, he was loved by none.

Pareto died on August 19, 1923. He lived a long and fruitful life in some of the most intellectually vibrant communities in Europe. Spending his final years in a picturesque village of his choosing, he is hardly to be pitied. But he did suffer the pain of having his most important works ignored or rejected by his contemporaries. Pareto was certain that he had laid the groundwork for the scientific study of society. He seems to have been equally convinced that intellectuals of his time were incapable of grasping the significance of his discoveries.

One can only wonder in dismay at the fact that so little progress has been made in the social sciences since Pareto's time. Few people are willing to follow his lead. While there are many good students, philosophers, and historians of society, there are a paltry few who can lay claim to the title "social scientist" the way Pareto meant it. That title must be reserved for those who, like Pareto himself, regard the development of a science based on discoverable laws of social organization as a realistic prospect.

Notes

1. Also see Charles Powers, "Pareto's Theory of Society," *Revue européenne des sciences sociales et Cahiers Vilfredo Pareto* 19 (December 1981): 99-119; three chapters on Pareto written by Powers, Turner, and Beeghley in *The Emergence of Sociological Theory* (Homewood, Ill.: Dorsey, 1981); and Charles Powers and Robert Hanneman, "Pareto's Theory of Social and Economic Cycles: A Formal Model and Simulation, *Sociological Theory* 1 (1983): 59-89.
2. Biographical information has been gleaned from a variety of sources. These include: Norberto Bobbio, *On Mosca and Pareto* (Geneva: Librairie Droz, 1972); Placido

Bucolo, *The Other Pareto* (New York: St. Martin's Press, 1980); S. E. Finer, "Pareto and Pluto-Democracy: The Retreat to Galapagos," *American Political Science Review* 62 (1968): 440-50; Arthur Livingston, "Bibliographic Note," in Vilfredo Pareto, *The Mind and Society* (New York: Harcourt, Brace, 1935), pp. xv-xviii; Maffeo Pantaleoni, "Vilfredo Pareto," *Economic Journal* 33 (September 1923): 582-90; Joseph Schumpeter, "Vilfredo Pareto, 1848-1923," *The Quarterly Journal of Economics* 63 (May 1949): 147-73; Vincent Tarascio, *Pareto's Methodological Approach to Economics* (Chapel Hill: University of North Carolina Press, 1966).
3. Vilfredo Pareto, "Principi fondamentali della teoria della elasticità de' corpi solidi e ricerche sulla integrazione delle equazioni differenziali che ne definiscono l'equilibrio," originally published in 1869, reprinted in Vilfredo Pareto, *Scritti teorici* (Milan: Malfasi, 1952), pp. 593-639.
4. For a selection of these essays, see Vilfredo Pareto, *La Liberté économique et les événements d'Italie* (New York: Burt Franklin, 1968).
5. This was a timely invitation because Pareto had vowed to leave Italy in order to escape political harassment.
6. Vilfredo Pareto, *Cours d'économie politique* (Lausanne: Rouge, 1896-97).
7. Translated into English as Vilfredo Pareto, *The Rise and Fall of the Elites* (Totowa, N.J.: Bedminster, 1968), introduced by Hans Zetterberg.
8. Vilfredo Pareto, *Les Systèmes socialistes* (Geneva: Librairie Droz, 1965, originally published in 1902-03).
9. Vilfredo Pareto, *Manual of Political Economy* (New York: August M. Kelley, 1971, trans. from 1909 rev. ed.).
10. Pareto's *Trattato di sociologia generale* was initially published in English as *The Mind and Society* (New York: Harcourt, Brace, 1935).
11. Norberto Bobbio, *On Mosca and Pareto* (Geneva: Librairie Droz, 1972), p. 45.
12. Pareto is credited with the concept of system in the introduction of Talcott Parsons's classic work *The Social System* (New York: Free Press, 1951). Parsons's later works, utilizing the concept of functional subsystems more completely, are even more indicative of Pareto's influence. For an informative study of Pareto's impact on the American social sciences during the first half of the twentieth century, see Barbara Heyl, "The Harvard 'Pareto Circle,'" *Journal of the History of the Behavioral Sciences* 4 (1968): 316-34.
13. For more detail, see Charles H. Powers, "Pareto's Theory of Society," *Revue européenne des sciences sociales et Cahiers Vilfredo Pareto* 19 (December 1981): 99-119.
14. Vilfredo Pareto, *Trasformazione della democrazia* (Milan: Corbaccio, 1921).
15. Pareto identified this paper as an October work, although it was actually completed in early November.
16. Norberto Bobbio, *On Mosca and Pareto* (Geneva: Librairie Droz, 1972), p. 52.
17. Benito Mussolini (1883-1945), dictator of fascist Italy, took power on October 22, 1922. Whether Pareto endorsed Mussolini remains a subject of debate.

1

Generalizations

The Transformation of Democracy is an imprecise title. But we will utilize it here for lack of a better one.

To begin with, the term "democracy" lacks definite meaning, as do many other terms borrowed from vulgar language. Sumner Maine sought to avoid definitional problems by replacing it with the term "popular government," and he published a book under this title.[1] But this second term is no more definitive than the first. Nor should we entertain any hope of finding terminology for a more rigorous and precise expression of a condition which is indeterminate and transitory.

The transformation from one state to another does not occur suddenly. Rather, there is continuous mutation similar to the process of evolutionary development in living creatures. We wish to study an aspect of this transformation.

Employing experimental method, we must not only reveal a sequence of change but also discover its correlates. If we were to do otherwise we would run the risk of supplanting objective research with subjective explanations reflecting our biases.

Two difficulties arise at this point. First, social processes take a long time to complete. My previous effort to conduct this kind of inquiry fills *Treatise on General Sociology*. I will therefore be obliged to make frequent reference to that work.[2] And in order to save readers from having to familiarize themselves with that work in complete detail, I will preface this study with some relevant findings. The second difficulty comes from the fact that a large number of historical documents are available for analysis. The volume of previous work, even restricting our attention to transformations of "popular governments" of which the present European transformation is a subset, is monumental.[3] Even this limited focus would be a broad topic for treatment in the space available. So it will be necessary to be brief and summarize. I will therefore need to limit myself to a few examples.

Many good books are available to readers wishing to study this topic in greater detail. Surely, I would not be so presumptuous as to compete with them. On the contrary, if I fail to cite them all here it is for lack of space rather than to conceal my indebtedness. And it is also because I intend to avoid writing a history of thought on the subject. Nor will I be restrained by the reverence I owe a master. If I note the disjunctions between a master's theories and the facts it is because concern with fact must direct all scholars following the precepts of experimental method.

Let us recall some general principles drawn from *Treatise on General Sociology*. We have to study the substance of events. We must assess how events have been viewed by people and discern the patterns of reasoning to which those events have given rise.

Sentiments and interests are the most constant and therefore the most important elements constituting the substance of phenomena (2146). Sentiments, and the residues which correspond to them, are analyzed in *Treatise on General Sociology*.[4] Material interests and the analysis of political economy are also discussed in that work.

The manifestations of sentiments and interests can vary, as do their logical consequences. These manifestations and consequences have typically been subjects of study by historians. Among the modern branches of history, those which inquire into the origins of institutions are very valuable.

Men view facts through their own prejudices. And if civilized people no longer believe that the sun plunges into the ocean every evening, they harbor other beliefs which are equally unrealistic. Moreover, it is natural for people to speculate about why things happen as well as how they happen. Logical-experimental science enables us to answer such questions within certain limits. But men show disdain for contingency and refuse to accept such limits. They aim instead for answers which are absolute. And since people rarely approach the study of social topics experimentally, pseudoscience replaces real science in the search for the absolute answers people crave. Interpretation of facts is determined by sentiments, desires, prejudices, and interests which often unknowingly motivate action. It is in this way that products of thought which we called "derivations" in *Treatise on General Sociology* have their origins.[5] None of these factors have any bearing on logical-experimental science.

Derivations are highly variable. They are often multicolored and fleeting like a rainbow. They simultaneously embody and obscure underlying social facts. We studied these facts in *Treatise on General Sociology* by analyzing the essence of derivations.

Neither metaphysics, which has absolute principles, nor empiricism, which is satisfied with superficial resemblances, are concerned with providing accurate analysis. Empiricists, in order to explain existing phenomena, look for past phenomena which are exactly alike. But like phenomena are not and cannot be found because history never really recurs. Infinite combinations can arise from the elements of human action, and history only chronicles such combinations.

Social order is never perfectly still: it is in perpetual motion. But metamorphosis can occur at different speeds. It can be observed in ancient times in Sparta as well as in Athens, and in modern times in China as well as in England. The difference is that change can occur at a slow pace as in Sparta or China, or motion can proceed quickly as in Athens or England. Moreover, such differences can characterize the same country at different points in time. For instance, Italy has experienced perpetual motion from the legendary times of Romulus until the present, but the process of change is more intense some years than others.

It is easy to understand how people mark the dawn of a new age. The coming of Christ marks the beginning of a new age for Christians, Hegira for Muslims,[6] the French Revolution of 1789 for believers in "democratic" religions, Lenin's revolution for a fervent believer in the Third International, and so on.[7] Practitioners of logical-experimental science should not dispute such claims because they are matters of faith and go completely beyond the experimental field. But if, from a logical-experimental point of view, one considers events only as facts without taking into account the adherence to faith they engender, it must be acknowledged that historical periods differ only in specifics. In their substance, events correspond to the peaks on a continuous curve. Reasoning from the peak downward, there was a Christianity before Christ, an Islam before Mohammed, a "democracy" before the French Revolution and a Bolshevism before Lenin's revolution.

It is useful to distance oneself from precast beliefs and examine events in this way, for detachment is indispensable in experimental science, but questioning faith very often impedes action. Although skepticism spawns theorizing, faith motivates people into the action that practical life requires. Ideals can be absurd and yet very useful for a society. We will have to frequently remind ourselves of this because the fact is easily neglected.

Maintaining a distinction between what is good for experimental science and what is good for society is fundamental. I wrote about that at length in *Treatise on General Sociology*. It must be mentioned again here in order to avoid the risk that some readers may interpret my observations of fact and relations among facts as advocacy of a particular state of affairs. This has often happened to me in the past. If I think I can conclude from historical facts that our bourgeoisie is running toward its ruin, that does not mean that I judge this trend to be "right" or "wrong." Neither would I evaluate the ruin of feudal lords, brought on by the Crusades, as good or bad. I would not exhort the bourgeoisie to change its path or preach for the reform of customs, tastes, or prejudices. Nor, even less, would I lead people to believe that I have a recipe to cure the illness from which the bourgeoisie or the wider society suffers. Quite the opposite. I declare explicitly that any such remedy, granted for the sake of argument, is completely unknown to me. I am like the physician who recognizes that the patient has tuberculosis but who does not know how to cure it. Let me add that, until the social sciences advance further, empiricists and practical men will have more insight into cures for the social organism than will physicians and scientists, even though the former can sometimes draw upon the knowledge of the latter.

Rationalism, as one of the intellectual "religions," reinforces the position that there should not be a distinction between theory and practice, a distinction between what is logically possible and faith in the impossible or fantastic, or a distinction between real goals and ideal goals. Rationalism suggests that one should work to make these distinctions disappear. So be it, but I study what is and not what "should be." And when men's sentiments, tastes, interests, and patterns of behavior will change, then the explanations we concoct will change, but not before (2411).

Only one objection might be raised. If a new order were impending, we would sense its arrival and would therefore be in a position to consider it scientifically. But there is no indication that the pattern of unfolding events which has been observed for more than two thousand years is likely to end. Let us then leave the trouble of studying the sociology of men of the distant future to our descendants and satisfy ourselves with sociology of men of the past, present, and near future.

The number of people agreeing with this position is growing smaller even as I write. And adherents may completely disappear now that I am about to illustrate the operation of my theoretical principles. Yet, I cannot conceal these consequences.

The first consequence is that one must decline making absolute judgments and be content with making contingent judgments. Every state results from past states and constitutes an origin for future states. Those who would like to pronounce an absolute judgment of "good" or "bad" should be familiar with all the future states which spring from the current state of affairs.[8] And since this is not possible, one must decline from making absolute judgments and be content with contingent judgments. People can only define "good" and "bad" by examining the "proximate" effects of a state of affairs under study and by setting limits to the term "proximate" [realizing that long-term trends often produce very different results].

Were the proscriptions of Roman Triumvirates, or the terror of the early period of the first French Revolution, or the terror of the Bolsheviks "good things" or "bad things"? This question can only be answered in terms of sentiments and faith which have their basis in a priori reasoning, metaphysical concepts, etc. The question cannot be answered in terms of logical-experimental science.

A rough concept of interdependence of historical phenomena is apparent in Clemenceau's assertion that one must consider the French Revolution in total (as a block) and that those who accept a part of it must accept it all.[9] Here one can clearly see the difference between a scientific explanation and a *derivation*. If Clemenceau wanted to be logical he would have had to extend this principle to the Russian Revolution. But on the contrary, Clemenceau fails, without giving any explanation, to consider the Russian Revolution as a "block." He condemns it because of its "terror" while refusing to condemn the French Revolution for exactly the same reason.

We can take this opportunity to observe that the case just mentioned is one particular example of a more general phenomenon [the use of derivations to justify a course of action]. One can say very little new about social facts that recur in every era because they have, in all probability, already made an impression on intelligent men. The difference between these prior impressions and our scientific vantage point can only be that science offers a closer approximation to experimental truth.

Let us construct an analogy. Ignorant men explain "rich" and "poor" soil differently than do chemists. Chemists know and ignorant men ignore the elements of which different types of soil are composed. However, chemists consider the terms "rich" and "poor" acceptable and precise. But ignorant men feel that these terms lack precision and should be discarded in rigorous scientific discussion. It would be nonsense to neglect the scientific advances made in chemistry or to say that chemists merely plagiarize from common sense. Nor is it correct to argue, as some supposed "gentlemen" do, that each new social theory has been copied from past authors. Some go so far as to suggest that Aristotle anticipated Darwin's theories.

A concept of economic oscillation can be found in the biblical story about seven fat cows and seven skinny cows, as well as in Clement Juglar's work on economic crises. But the approximation of these theories to reality is inadequate. The concept of oscillation in the character of society as a whole can be found in the approximations of Vico's metaphysical theory, in Ferrari's theory,[10] or in modern logical-experimental science.[11]

The careful study of facts teaches us a very important lesson. It is that "oscillations of the various parts of the social whole are interdependent. These oscillations are simply the manifestations of changes within the parts themselves.[12] If one insisted on using the misleading term 'cause' one could say that the descending period is the cause of the ascending period that follows, and vice versa. But this is only in the sense that the ascending period is indissolubly joined with the descending period which precedes it, and vice versa. Generally, therefore, different periods are only the manifestations of stages in a single cycle. Observation reveals that periods succeed one another, and to follow this succession is to discover an experimental uniformity. Oscillations vary according to the length of time required for their completion. Oscillations can be very short, short, long, or very long" (2338). Therefore, we must determine whether the transformation we now face will be a brief oscillation in response to ephemeral events, or a moderate movement, or a major change in cyclical events (1718).

A second consequence is drawn from the observation that a search for the most "outstanding" form of government is vain and fanciful. This follows from the indeterminate nature of the term "outstanding" (2110). It also follows from the fact that an impossible event is implicitly assumed to be possible, that is, it is assumed that the process of change slows in favor of good government.

One also confronts serious difficulties because the social sciences have failed to advance very far. On the other hand, one might hope that we will partially overcome obstacles that obscure uniformities from view and obscure the nature of interdependence among social facts.

If we turn our attention to the numerous theories about constitutional and parliamentary states articulated during the last century, it becomes clear that none of them can be applied to contemporary events. Those theories point in one direction and the facts point in the opposite direction. For instance, Mill's *Considerations on Representative Government* and *Essays on Liberty*, books that were once very famous, strike readers as being completely divorced from the reality of contemporary England.

Who is now interested in theories of equilibrium of power? Who determines the correct equilibrium between State's rights and individual rights? Can an Ethical State of which people speak so respectfully (despite obvious irony), really be found? Certainly, the Hegelian State is the product of a very vivid imagination and yet has survived wear and tear of poetic and metaphysical sociology. Working people are more interested in the tangible benefits of high wages, progressive taxes, and increased leisure time than in metaphysics; although it must be admitted that workers avoid showing disdain for their own myths about proletarian virtue, the evil of the capitalist order (1890), the desirability of worker democracy, and so on.

We were once told that war was impossible because advances in deadly military technology made conflict unthinkable. At the worst, war was to be averted at the last minute thanks to a general strike or some other plan of workers and, especially, socialists. What hypocrites! Such nice speeches did nothing to stop the outbreak of World War I. No general strike materialized. On the contrary, socialist parliamentarians in the different countries either supported war appropriations or failed to oppose them in any significant way. German Socialists, Marx's heirs, voted almost unanimously for war appropriations. The precept of the master: "Proletarians of the world, unite!" was then implicitly transformed into: "Proletarians of the world, kill one another."

Now [1920] myths and prophecies are being renewed. Some say that the League of Nations represents the triumph "of the defenders of goodness and justice" (others would even add "liberty") and that the League will bring peace and joy to the world. Still other people believe that Bolshevism will bring that same peace and joy to the world. Certainly, a number of them do not really believe what they say, but many others are quite sincere and have the conviction which faith provides. Even if it may seem strange, there are still those who are persuaded, despite recent disappointing events, that the League of Nations will cure all the ills of the world. There are those, although they are few, who keep faith with Wilson's Fourteen Points.[13] More than any previous thinker, Wilson was able to isolate the foundations for a good republic. He may be right. There are still those who believe in magic, and it is said that there are even some people who invoke the devil. Moreover, consider how numerous are believers in Christian Science.

Let us continue with the third consequence. When one assesses any act to determine whether it is "good, fair, equitable, moral, religious, patriotic, etc.," one really seeks to determine if the action is consistent with the sentiments of some collectivity at a given point in time. Such sentiments tend to be vaguely defined. This can be useful if one needs collective consensus, but it says little or nothing about the possibility of putting policies into practice or what the economic and social consequences of such policies might be.

The fact that a concept has survived in a society for a long time shows that it is compatible with societal conditions. Consequently, it is possible that by measuring such a concept one also measures societal conditions (1778, 2520). But anything can be shown to be true if inadequate measures are employed.

For instance, knowing that the Crusade to Asia to free Christ's Holy Sepulcher would be interpreted as a religious act would have allowed one to forecast the warm welcome extended to the Crusaders by those local Christians who were deeply religious.[14] But this knowledge would not have allowed one to predict the economic, political, and social consequences of the Crusades. A baron who took part in a crusade was supposedly a good Christian, although perhaps mainly a restless adventurer. But he was surely a bad feudal lord because he prepared for the ruin of his caste. The capitalists of our time, who are so eager to make war, are supposedly good patriots, although there are some profiteers among them. But they are, in part, producing the next destruction of their class.

In this and many similar cases, if one estimates the social usefulness of a course of action, one can say that people who contribute to that work are people who follow in pursuit of an ideal goal. They often unknowingly follow a track they would not have followed had they known where the track led.

Therefore, it is one thing to reason about ideal ends and another thing to assess real patterns of change. The divine right of kings and emperors, the sacrosanct power of the majority, and the divine right of workers can all be defended with excellent arguments. In the same way, Pobedonostzeff had excellent arguments to exalt Tsarist autocracy.[15] What malarkey! It contributes nothing to our understanding of the consequences of different government policies.

Sparta forbade citizenship to strangers. Rome bestowed it indirectly by welcoming freemen among its citizens. How can one assess such measures? First, they can be assessed from the standpoint of supposed equality among men, of protection of inalienable rights, and of humanity. Second, they can be assessed from the standpoint of economic, social, and political consequences. These are two different issues which have nothing in common with one another.

Is a tax "fair" or "unfair"? One possible approach is to answer this question in terms of sentiments. Hence, the arguments one invokes in a discussion of the subject are only *derivations*. Another possible approach is to answer this question in terms of formal logic. In that case, the question is only answerable if one knows what meanings the terms "fair" and "unfair" have. Less than 100 years have gone by since a time when it was considered "unfair" for a tax to be levied by anyone other than those paying that tax. In fact, for centuries people accepted the maxim that the consensus of taxpayers is necessary if taxes are to be considered "fair." This was the foundation of the House of Commons in England and of other analogous conventions. Even progressive taxes which provided a way of taking money away from the "well-to-do" and giving it to the "poor," some of whom live better than the well-to-do, were thought of as "unfair." Those progressive taxes result in a drain on capital, etc. Now [1920] progressive taxes are considered proper and just. So there is nothing to discuss in the issue of "fairness" inasmuch as it depends exclusively on the meanings one imputes to the terms being employed. But the syllogisms one may use to address the question of fairness will prove useless in solving the second question, which is an entirely different issue. What economic, political, and social consequences will policies have?[16]

It may be "fair, praiseworthy, desirable, morally necessary" that workers be allowed to work short hours and draw enormous wages. But the issue of fairness differs from the question of practicality. First, is it practical to think that real rather than nominal wages will be granted? Second, what consequences would such a state of affairs have?

Perhaps some readers will be scandalized by such assertions and will consider them heretical. Conversely, others will judge them so evident as to obviate the need for their expression. I will remind the first category of readers that my objective is to perform an exclusively experimental study free of the tethers of faith. I will remind the second category of readers that a great many people, far from considering such assertions evident, think they are absurd falsehoods. Therefore, it is not at all useless to stand aloof from those people.

Let us go on with other heresies. Determining what indemnity Germany "must" pay after its defeat was a legal exercise—more accurately a pseudological exercise—in international morality, equity, etc. Determining how to exact an indemnity without using that term, because using the term would hurt Wilson, exemplifies the use of *derivations*. But all this cannot substitute, as far as practical effects are concerned, for efforts to determine what Germany "can" pay and what is "useful" for the winners to ask.

Two operations help in forecasting events. First, an observer inquires into possibilities. Second, the observer calculates the probability of different outcomes. The past provides examples of what is possible (134), or more precisely, experimental observation suggests that some things are logically dependent on elements being observed. The likelihood of particular outcomes can be

Generalizations 33

extrapolated from general uniformities observed over time in different places (556 and following). These two inquiries must, for the above reasons, turn toward the less variable elements of phenomena rather than the complex events [involving random and idiosyncratic details] which empiricists often treat. This is true for an excellent reason. There is no use in looking for a predictable pattern that does not exist.

During the nineteenth century, many people applied the so-called historical method to the study of social phenomena. And a number of important inquiries were made concerning the origins of these phenomena. This represented notable progress in getting closer to experience, when compared with the kinds of ethical and metaphysical analysis which were once, and in some respects continue, to be important (857 and following). But we can improve upon historicism by employing a genuinely experimental methodology.

An institution or a social fact observable in a given period can be, but is not necessarily, a direct transformation of a prior institution or social fact. However, evolution tends not to follow a straight line (217) and sharing common elements should not be confused with proof of origin of descent. When considering birds and mammals as classes, birds of prey and felines can be said to occupy analogous positions. But not even the most extreme Darwinist would argue that felines evolved from birds of prey. Contemporary unions are analogous to gilds of the Middle Ages. But even if some fervent adherents of the method of social origins once viewed it as a case of direct descent, others were more cognizant of experience and resolutely rejected the descent thesis.

Metaphysicians start with absolute principles and attempt to develop explanations of reality that are consistent with those principles. Experimental scientists begin with real facts and seek to discover common properties and patterns, also called abstractions. Experimental abstraction has nothing to do with metaphysical abstraction.

I mention this because there are authors who confuse metaphysics and experimental method. Their ignorance of the distinctions between the two follows from lack of familiarity with experimental method.

The degree to which one can engage in experimental abstraction is infinite. Every general principle can depend upon one even more general, and so on, without limit. But following this track is not always useful or suitable to our purposes. One should avoid the risk of generalizing beyond the boundaries of present experience and roaming in imaginary space. It was appropriate for Newton to limit himself to consideration of the gravitational universal, while it is appropriate for modern engineers to want to progress further, and it will be appropriate for people of the future to move beyond modern advances. One should also take careful notice of the fact that it is important to be able to restrict one's own research. Newton's followers performed a very useful service by limiting their studies to consequences of the principle of gravitation.

They would have contributed little had they searched only for "the essence" of gravitation. Similarly, there seems to be growing interest in idle discussion of "values" among some economists (if they can be called economists.)[17]

In *Treatise on General Sociology* we analyzed elements called "residues." There is no doubt that this term covers an endless series of widely observable facts and that, sooner or later, we will discover even more general facts. *Everything* may eventually be explainable in that way. It would be a blatant contradiction if one were to argue that experimental method never yields absolute knowledge, while at the same time arguing that all phenomena can be explained in terms of discoverable principles. I will now speak only for myself and not for others. Let us see what insights can be drawn from widely observable facts. This task is more exhausting, more modest, more prosaic, but yet much more useful than allowing our imagination to wander in infinite space beyond the realm of experience. As I have already said, this approach is valid if regarded from a scientific standpoint. But it is not valid if regarded from the standpoint of faith, which pushes common people to action.

Those who argue that scientific reasoning is less important than faith in motivating people are correct. I do not want to dispute that. So they are justified in the study which they consider to be of principal importance, and may be content that [my effort to construct] logical-experimental theory is among the studies of secondary importance.

In order to discover elements relevant to the question we ask, let us search for other analogous facts. We will find different facts regarding different elements. Those who carefully observe facts as they are now unfolding will notice at least three very distinct trends: (1) the weakening of central authority and growth in the forces of anarchy, (2) rapid movement on a cycle of demagogic plutocracy, and (3) the transformation of sentiments of the bourgeoisie and of the class that still rules.

These three trends are the subjects of the essays to follow.

Notes

This chapter was originally published May 5, 1920 in *Rivista di Milano*. The chapters that follow appeared in monograph form as *Trasformazione della democrazia* (Milan: Corbaccio, 1921).
1. Sir Henry James Sumner Maine, 1822-1888, was an English jurist and historian known for his works on the history of law and the history of civilization, including *Ancient Law* (1861) and *Popular Government: Four Essays* (1885).[Ed.]
2. I will do this by using parentheses to note the numbers of *passages*, rather than page numbers, from *Treatise on General Sociology*.
3. Pareto refers at different times to three transformations in government: (1) the transformation of democracy into demagogic plutocracy, (2) the transformation of demagogic plutocracy into military plutocracy, and (3) the transformation of military plutocracy into democracy. In Pareto's view, these transformations were the empirical manifestations of a balance between the countervailing forces of centralization and decentralization of power. Strong central control generates

forces of resistance which take form in calls for democratization and decentralized control. But wily elites are able to deceive the masses and manipulate democratic forms of government for their own advantage. The trend toward decentralization accelerates with the rise of demagogic plutocracy, and, as the power of the central government becomes more and more tenuous, the social fabric begins to disintegrate. It is at this point that pressure for centralization mounts and forceful leaders emerge to reestablish central authority. Thus, each transformation was regarded by Pareto as part of a recurring plutocratic cycle. These chapters are intended as a specific case study of a portion (and only a portion) of that cycle as it unfolded in Italy around 1920.[Ed.]
4. "Sentiments" are subconscious beliefs which serve as standards of evaluation. "Residues" are behavioral manifestations reflecting the sentiments people have.[Ed.]
5. "Derivations" are ex post facto accounts people devise in order to make past events seem natural, logical, reasonable, or just.[Ed.]
6. Hegira refers to Mohammed's flight from Mecca to Medina in June, 622.[Ed.]
7. Pareto regards blind faith as the distinguishing characteristic of religion. Consequently, he places in one common category all those movements and memberships resting upon faith. He labels these "religions" in order to accentuate their commonality. According to Pareto, belief in a metaphysical principle (e.g. equality) provides believers with much the same kind of phenomenological experience that faith in a deity does.[Ed.]
8. See *Treatise on General Sociology*, 2238, 2548 (B2).
9. George Clemenceau, 1841-1921, was French Premier during 1906-09 and 1917-19. He was defeated in the elections of 1919 because it was widely felt that he was soft on Germany in the aftermath of World War I.[Ed.]
10. Giovanni Battista Vico, 1668-1744, was an Italian philosopher and jurist who attempted the scientific study of history. He is known for his cyclical theory of history—that society moves inexorably through stages of theocracy, aristocracy, and democracy because each stage contains the seeds of its own destruction. Giuseppe Ferrari, 1812-1876, was a political philosopher who advocated Italian federalism and opposed Cavour's plan for national unification under a monarchy.[Ed.]
11. See *Treatise on General Sociology*, 2330.
12. Pareto is referring to his concept of cyclical change. A set of dynamics intrinsic to the economy make oscillation between periods of expansion and contraction inevitable. A set of dynamics intrinsic to the political sphere make oscillation between periods of centralization and erosion of central power inevitable. A set of dynamics intrinsic to popular sentiment make oscillation between periods of faith and skepticism inevitable. And each of these cycles interacts with one another, accounting for patterns of change in the society as a whole.[Ed.]
13. The "Fourteen Points" were President Woodrow Wilson's proposals for promoting international reconciliation in the aftermath of World War I.[Ed.]
14. The Holy Sepulcher is the Church of the Resurrection, constructed in Jerusalem on the site Saint Helen identified as the location of Jesus' tomb.[Ed.]
15. Pareto is probably referring to Konstantin Petrovich Pobyedonostzev, 1827-1907. Pobyedonostzev was Protector of the Holy Synod (1880-1905). He was a conservative, advocated Russification, and supported the persecution of nonconformists.[Ed.]

16. Interest in this subject is now being rekindled among economists. See the very important studies by Guido Sensini and Gino Borgatta, published in *Giornale degli Economisti* (1920).
17. A "value" as an abstraction deduced from facts has nothing to do with a "value" defined as a metaphysical entity which dominates facts and is assumed to explain them. People who do not understand this do not understand anything about experimental method.

2

The Crumbling of Central Authority

In every human collectivity two forces are in conflict. Centripetal force encourages the concentration of central power. Centrifugal force fosters the erosion of power.

Let us briefly refer to *Treatise on General Sociology*. The aim of this digression is to explain the relationship between "residues" and the centripetal and centrifugal forces under examination.

Centripetal and centrifugal forces are chiefly influenced by the strength of traditional attachments. They are also affected by residues of sociality. Under certain conditions centrifugal force grows and centripetal force is diminished. Centrifugal tendencies grow during periods of increasing communalism and particularism, and during periods of declining religious strength and diminishing desire for uniformity.

We know that "residues" change in a wave-like manner over time. Therefore, we can forecast similar wave-like movement in the centripetal and centrifugal forces powering centralization and decentralization of power. Since centripetal and centrifugal forces undergo perpetual change, the equilibrium point marking their balance also oscillates over time. But successive cycles are not regular or identical. Each new oscillation manifests itself differently.

The feudal period during Europe's Middle Ages reflects this kind of cyclical change. In France there were actually two cycles during the feudal period. A long cycle was preceded by a shorter cycle. The centralized power of the Merovingian monarchy crumbled at the same time that the Carolingian government rose. Strong central government was reconstituted under Carolingian rule, but under the last sovereigns of their stock it too crumbled away. Another period of centralization did not begin until the rise of the kings of France.

Analogous cycles can be isolated if one studies the general history of various countries and epochs. When we identify the "feudal" period we are actually using an inclusive term to cover a broad period in which more than one cycle occurred.

We have observed that feudal organization rose and then declined. That is to say that dynamic phenomena or, more precisely, cyclical phenomena were occurring.

In this sense, Vico's theory of the recurrence of lord and vassal relationships is accurate. But he errs both in assuming that successive oscillations have identical form and in his imaginatively inaccurate descriptions of events. Following in this direction would lead us out of the experimental field.

Countless theories could be used to account for the historical facts of the European feudal period. I do not have the slightest intention of reviewing these theories, for this would not contribute to the objective I have in mind in writing this paper. Nor is there sufficient space for such a review. But it will be useful to consider some examples in order to demonstrate that different theories share important elements in common.

Montesquieu interprets the phenomenon already noted as a case of unilinear evolutionary development. He argues that vassalage originated in ancient Germany. Vassalage is then said to have undergone a series of changes which gave rise to feudalism. Germans naturally favor such theories because men tend to prefer *derivations* which are consistent with their sentiments. Latin authors accept the theory of direct evolution as well. But they favor theories which identify Rome as the cradle of civilization. They identify *precarium* and clientage as the original roots from which feudalism developed.[1] Rather than informing us about the true origins of feudalism, these derivations merely tell us what the people in each society want to hear. We also see this in Falch's theory. He identifies the "clan" as the origin from which feudal society developed in the eleventh and twelfth centuries.

Consider another illustration. The critical dimension of Pertile's theory is insightful, although the positive dimension is not. He writes (203-4):

> Let us not mention Vico's eternal law of feudal relations. Feudal relations did not originate in the clientage found in ancient Roman law or in military benefices of the empire. Neither of these factors had much to do with feudal relations. [This may be true. However, one should add that they manifest forces which operate in a similar way.][2] One finds a personal relationship of protection or defense in clientage. Vassalage is a similar relationship involving respect and services. On the other hand, clientage begot even greater effects than vassalage. It involved the intergenerational transmission of name and hereditary rights between clients and patrons. [The difference is one of form rather than of substance, as noted in *Treatise on General Sociology*, 1039.] On the contrary, the essence of feudalism, and with it the military aspect of feudalism, is found in imperial benefices. A personal element does not appear in these benefices. [Pertile should have recognized such circumstances as subsidiary.] In fact military service was owed the state rather than the prince. [There is slight difference when the prince is the state.] Moreover, feudal relations cannot be said to originate in these institutions because they are not linked by developmental continuity. [This case illustrates that evolution is not unilinear.] Feudal relations are frequently said to have their origins in events during the barbaric period. But barbarian and feudal relations have nothing in common. Feudal relations involve lands given as full property and do not impose a legal relationship between the king and the owner of lands. Feudal relations do not even impose the obligation of maintaining a militia on the land holder. [This position is

technically correct but may be overstated.] None of the other Lombardic or Merovingian land assignments had the character of benefices, so that one is encouraged to set back the origin of feudalism to the time of the barbarian conquests. . . . Some authors still believe that feudalism evolved in this way. In this genesis, feudal relations were not originally revocable at will. Later they were revocable yearly. Still later they were lifelong, and they finally became hereditary.[3]

We find analogous theories to explain the development of contemporary trade unions. There are those who look to Roman corporations for the origins of trade unions. Others begin their search more discretely with medieval gilds or associations of wage earners. Sidney and Beatrice Webb properly refuse to utilize such theories in their history of trade unionism (1894:11-13).

We have dwelt at some length upon these ephemeral associations of wage earners and on the journeymen fraternities of the Middle Ages, because it might plausibly be argued that they were in some sense the predecessors of the Trade Union. But strangely enough it is not in these institutions that the origin of Trade Unionism has usually been sought. For the predecessor of the modern Trade Union, men have turned, not to the medieval associations of the wage-earners, but to those of their employers—that is to say, the Craft Gilds. The outward resemblance of the Trade Union to the Craft Gild had long attracted the attention, both of the friends and the enemies of Trade Unionism.[4]

This is a mistake commonly made by empiricists, who stop with a superficial analysis of facts rather than isolating the more constant patterns which are discoverable.

But it was the publication in 1870 of Professor Brentano's brilliant study on the "Origin of Trade Unions" that gave form to the popular idea. . . . And when Mr. George Howell prefixed to his history of Trade Unionism a paraphrase of Dr. Brentano's account of the Gilds, it became accepted that the Trade Union had, in some undefined way, really originated from the Craft Gild. . . . The supposed descent of the Trade Unions from the medieval Craft Gild rests, as far as we have been able to discover, upon no evidence whatsoever. The historical proof is all the other way.

Sidney and Beatrice Webb are inclined to attribute the origin of trade unions to "the divorce of the worker from the ownership of the means of production" (1894:35). But they wisely add that they "do not contend that the divorce supplies, in itself, a complete explanation of the origin of Trade Unions" (1894:37).

One should not look to social theories for true origins of unionism. Rather, the opposite is true. Similarly, theories of feudalism reflect the consequences rather than the causes of feudal relations. The same can also be said about theories of royal power. These theories are consequences rather than causes for the rise of royal power and the decline of semi-autonomous fiefdoms. But I do not deny that theories help to further accentuate phenomena after the theories are initially articulated. I simply deny that theories capture the main cause of the phenomena they are intended to explain. Therefore, I embrace rather than reject the opinion that myths are effective in pressing men into action. Sorel demonstrates this in detail. I only deny that the myths are guides to adequate understanding of observable reality.

Sidney and Beatrice Webb inform us of one case that is particularly important. This case substantiates the propositions demonstrated at length in *Treatise on General Sociology*. The Webbs (1894:47-48) refer to an important example from their own period, which is now in the past.

> The action of the House of Commons on occasions like these was not as yet influenced by any conscious theory of freedom or contract. . . . That the House of Commons remained innocent of any theory against legislative interference long after it had begun the work of sweeping away the medieval regulations is proved by the famous case of Spitalfields silk weavers, in which the old policy of industrial regulation was reverted to. . . . Clearly the parliaments which passed the Spitalfields Acts of 1765 and 1773 had no conception of the political philosophy of Adam Smith, whose *Wealth of Nations* [which] afterwards proved to be accepted as the English gospel of freedom of contract and "natural liberty," was published in 1776. At the same time, so exceptional had such acts become, that when Adam Smith's masterpiece came into the hands of the statesmen of the time, it must have seemed not so much a novel view of industrial economics as the explicit generalization of practical conclusions to which experience had already repeatedly driven them. Towards the end of the century the governing classes, who had found in the new industrial policy a source of enormous pecuniary profit, eagerly seized on the new economic theory as an intellectual and moral justification of that policy.

This is just what leaders do now. They always have some theory they can use to their own advantage. At that time they used the theory of laissez-faire economics. Now it is unionist rhetoric that is popular. Tomorrow they will replace it with yet another doctrine that they find momentarily useful.

Agostino Lanzillo also argues that unions are the producers rather than the products of theory.

> European countries will have to solve the problems of being "warlike" and "mercantile," "democratic," and "militaristic." We do not know what the practical outcome of these competing demands will be. Will society be organized in terms of free trade or state socialism? Will new experiments imitate present regimes? What will be the *political* consequences of military exigencies? What will the fiscal consequences be? What forms will ideal, moral, and religious phenomena assume in this new age? There is an infinite array of possible questions. Trade unions will be able to perform a glorious task by contributing to the creation of a new ideology. Development of this new ideology is a *condition sine qua non* of the moral reinstatement of western countries after the devastating war.[5]

One could employ additional citations in order to further substantiate this position. The comments of A. O. Olivetti should be sufficient to conclude this point.

> Trade unionists do not want to impose solutions which were ready-made in Moscow and Leningrad. Trade unionism is revolutionary precisely because it matures with daily experience. Its aim is an organic revolution rather than an aprioristic one. Plans for reconstruction which are based on symmetrical fantasy are abhorrent.[6]

We have at least partly raised the veils that previously shrouded reality. Now let us return to our analysis of reality. In the passages that follow we will examine the moving equilibrium of centripetal and centrifugal forces between centralization and decentralization of power.

Central power is weakened during periods when centrifugal force gains momentum. It does not really matter whether the central power is monarchical, oligarchic, or popular in form. For "sovereignty" is a word that ceases to have much meaning as central power crumbles and covers the country with its debris. When central power crumbles the power of some individuals and some collectivities will grow. These collectivities remain subordinate in theory to the seat of central government. But in practice they gain autonomy. Those who do not belong to such collectivities are weak. No longer protected by the sovereign, they must look elsewhere for protection and adjudication. They can either trust a powerful patron, enter into secret or public partnerships with other weak people, or join associations, communes, or trade unions.

Movement in this direction inevitably generates a reaction in the opposite direction. Reaction occurs because protection gradually turns into subjugation. The number of adversaries to the existing order grows as a result. Under favorable social and, more importantly, economic conditions, adversaries grow in power as well as in number. At the same time, rivalries among loci of decentralized power grow as their fears of central power diminish. These rivalries frequently end in open conflict and anarchy. Centripetal force gains momentum under this combination of circumstances.

As a general rule, weak people need protection (2180), and they seek it from those who have power. They seek it from various lords when centrifugal force prevails and from the central government when centripetal force prevails. When circumstances favor centripetal force, the new or previously existing central government removes power from the hands of the dominant oligarchy and concentrates power in its own hands. Centralization of power can occur over short or long periods, and it can be gradual or abrupt and violent. One might note that this transformation is often followed by religious phenomena. This is what we saw in Europe at the end of the Middle Ages, in Russia at the time of Ivan the Terrible, in Japan in the nineteenth century, and in many other cases. This is not a coincidence but a natural consequence. The strengthening of religious sentiments is a manifestation of increasing traditionalism and "persistence of aggregates." These sentiments are the cement which binds human societies.

International conflicts also affect cyclical movements, both in centralization and decentralization of power. The defeat of a central power in a war can contribute to its downfall. Hence, military defeat favors centrifugal motion while victory can have the opposite effect. But victory does not always produce the same results. If victory is achieved at great cost and sacrifice, central power can also be weakened. This danger was more easily avoided when armies were smaller and doubled as work brigades, which is why the successors of Alexander the Great could fight among themselves. The Roman Empire, and more recently a number of European monarchies, could sustain the luxury of incessant wars that bled their people. But World War I involved such full mobilization at such great cost that it seriously shook central power in the victorious states as well as in the defeated nations.[7]

World War I had the effect of accelerating an evolution that would otherwise have occurred much more slowly. The empires of Russia, on one side, and of Germany and Austria-Hungary, on the other side, fell because they abrogated their agreements. These empires, sometimes referred to as conservative, would have been invincible had they remained united. Instead, they have been replaced by so-called democratic regimes. Now the demagogic plutocracy is tottering and the whole bourgeois order has been shaken. This is happening because of disagreements and war caused by excessive greed. Capitalists have employed the imperialist "religion" too excessively. Their positions would have been secure had they made peace in 1917, but one side insisted on total victory, and the other side would not admit to defeat. The adversaries of the bourgeoisie acted wisely in letting them writhe in vain with indissoluble difficulties.

There are many examples of similar waves. The equilibrium point between centripetal and centrifugal forces moves cyclically over time.

Central power was preponderant in Europe from 774 until 800. Charlemagne imposed his authority on the Church as well as on laymen. No one in his vast empire dared to oppose him. However, things changed soon after his passing, and Western Europe was reduced to a state of anarchy by the time the last Carolingian emperor died in 899. Thus, one cycle between centripetal and centrifugal force was essentially complete in a period of a little more than a century.

There are those who chose to view the Norman invasion as the cause of the disintegration of the Carolingian Empire, but this is not true. If it were true, then why would the fearful Saracen invasion have been instrumental in the foundation of such an empire?[8] The effects of foreign conflicts reinforce rather than dictate internal trends.

At the beginning of the nineteenth century centripetal force was on the ascent in England. Parliament was actually sovereign. People would have laughed had associations such as unions tried to oppose Parliamentary power. This would have been as ridiculous as a country squire confined to his manor trying to oppose Charlemagne's power. Today, little more than a century has passed since the time when Parliament was omnipotent. It was said that Parliament could do everything but change men into women, but this power has partially crumbled and vanished. Unions have inherited power and now negotiate on an equal footing with Parliament as well as the other arms of government.

The current state of affairs is reflected in a comment made by Lloyd George in the Commons on February 10, 1920. "The problems we are facing with a lack of cheap housing are caused by a scarcity of cheap labor. This scarcity can be traced to trade unions which prevent us from hiring the 350,000 people who are currently out of work." So the unemployed must have the permission of unions in order to work. Will Parliament protect their right to work? No. Lloyd George continued. "It is the position of the Labor Party that corporate interests should not be preferred to national interests." Until recently, insuring that private interests did not prevail over the common good was the concern of Parliament and not the concern of private associations.

This new trend has produced some strange consequences. In Italy consumption of meat on Fridays and Saturdays is forbidden in order to discourage depletion of livestock. People who eat steak on those days are punished, but union butchers are allowed to kill steers with impunity. Agricultural strikes happened to break out at the same time that the government decreed these hypocritical restrictions. Strikers prevented people from feeding and watering cattle before the very eyes of indulgent police. Even the owners were prevented from feeding their cattle. Moreover, the farm workers forbade the sale of these cattle for consumption.

Charlemagne's subjects were directly dependent upon him, as Emperor and as King of the Franks, and owed an oath of allegiance to him. He strengthened and widened his control by sending his *missi*, his messengers, all around the Empire.[9] They were charged "to carefully investigate whenever a citizen lodged complaint against an injustice." They were not to yield "because of adulation, reward, blood relationship, or fear of powerful people." Another capitulary reads:

> If by any chance some bishops or Counts neglect their duty they will be reprimanded by *missi*. All the people will know that anyone failing to obtain justice because of a Count's neglect, carelessness, or lack of power, can lodge a complaint and obtain justice with the help of *missi*. We encharge *missi* to adjudicate disputes when people turn to them out of necessity.[10]

Under Charlemagne's successors there were still some *missi dominici* or king's messengers. However, their power and importance gradually evaporated. Charles the Bald managed to send representatives asking nobles to respect his prohibition against the construction of new castles. But his was a vain menace. Castles grew in number and power as little local sovereigns arose from the ruins of central power.

One need not confuse the actual state with the ideal state or with the legal state. In France, the de facto authority of the king disappears with the coming of Capet [King of France, 987-996]. The ideal of absolute authority survived and would later be used to justify the revitalization of central power. But theories which suggest that centralization of power followed and was caused by development of the doctrine of absolute authority are incorrect. Such theories are polluted by a desire for an a priori explanation of facts in terms of ideas. On the contrary, experience teaches us that ideas are often the consequences of facts.

The evolutionary transformation of unions resembles the evolutionary transformation of feudalism. Therefore, examining the present transformation of unions enables us to understand the transformation of feudal relations. This is helpful since the transformation of feudal relations occurred in the distant past and is little known. On the other hand, what little we do know about past phenomena allows us to better conceptualize the pattern of contemporary events.

We can replace discussion of continuous transformations with discontinuous ones for the purpose of exposition. With this restriction in mind, we can accept the divisions in trade union history noted by Sidney and Beatrice Webb. They divide union history into six periods: (1) struggle for life 1799-1825, (2) a revolutionary period 1829-1842, (3) spiritual revival 1843-1860, (4) the period of Giunta and its allies 1860-1875, (5) old and new unionism 1875-1889, and (6) trade unionism after 1893.

One needs to add that the latest period continues until the beginning of World War I, and a new period begins with the end of that war. This could be a period of great ascendance for unions. Considerable progress has been made in the cause of unionism. Moreover, this progress is general since it has been observed in many countries. Erosion of central power has become apparent. Disparity between the ideology and the reality of political control is growing as a result.

Fustel de Coulanges disproves the thesis that feudal society began with the *Articles* of Kiersy in 877.[11] He provides an adequate treatment of changes in political ideology, but his account of the actual point of transformation into feudalism is lacking. He himself recognizes this.[12] On pages 474-75 he writes:

> Now that our analysis has restored the Articles of Kiersy to their true meaning, it is important to see if they have not had, as often occurs, a more vital importance than that which their author intended to give them. Let us first note the uses and practices which are contained in them. We will not speak of Article 1, which marks the great position the Church has made for herself in the state. [At present the Church has been replaced by socialism; especially by the turncoat kind of socialism.] It is not, moreover, an innovation. Nor will we say anything

about several articles, such as the second, fifth, and numbers eighteen through twenty-two, in which Charles the Bald, while speaking as master, reveals his fear of not being obeyed.

Similarly, our governments pass laws even if they know those laws will be disregarded by unions. For instance, most governments forbid strikes by civil servants. However, unions disregard such prohibitions. Under such circumstances governments often threaten to dismiss strikers but this tends to be an idle threat. Unions are also allowed to violate laws protecting private property. Like the man who fell off a horse and exclaimed, "I wanted to get off," government officials usually search for some way to rationalize union usurpation of private property.

> We will not dwell upon Article 18, by which the king feels the need to remind the counts that they are civil servants. But Article 4 and the response which is made in it by the great ones merit particular attention. In it the king and the faithful make pledges to one another. The king again pronounces the word "obedience;" but it is obvious that this is no longer a question of that general, obligatory obedience, superior to the wills, which subjects owe to a king in a monarchical state. It is only a question of that which a man owes to one to whom it has been promised. What is curious here is the simplicity with which these ideas are expressed as known truths. They seem banal, natural, and uncontested.

Today railroad employees pay even less attention to government proclamations than noblemen did to the decrees of Charles the Bald, and administrators and judges act as if they had forgotten their duties. The mutual pledge of obedience (Article 4) is exactly the kind of phenomenon we see now. Powerful unions such as the miners' union in England, and railroad unions in any country, are able to establish peace treaties with national governments. Another analogy with our situation can also be drawn. Our legislative assemblies have lost their omnipotent superiority just as the king once had. Allegiances which are "promised" rather than "owed" the king are analogous to the promises unions make to governments. Such promises are gratuitous and are only honored as long as it serves the interests of the unions. Similarly, the fact that unions negotiate with the government on an equal footing now strikes people as being natural. It is no longer subject to dispute. Railroad workers, who are paid by the state, can refuse to carry soldiers or police.[13] In this case we see rules analogous to *immunity* in the Middle Ages. If the analogy is not exact, it is at least conceptually correct. Railroad workers think, even if they have not clearly articulated the perception yet, that the power of the central government stops at the borders of their domain. Opinions which are more or less comparable are gaining currency in other unions.

The capacity of some people to avoid justice is a sure sign that central power is crumbling, just as the necessity of submitting to state jurisdiction

46 The Transformation of Democracy

is a sure sign of the ascendance of central power. Cyclical changes in the strength of central power precede changes in ideology and law.

We can see one such transformation occurring now. Union "immunity" has not yet assumed the kind of formal character church and lay "immunity" eventually gained under the Carolingians. But union "immunity" is gradually coming into being. A growing number of unions seem exempt from enforcement of laws and regulations. And the extension of "immunity" is supported, to some degree, by public opinion.

If the state were forced to change its laws, then there would at least be a formal recognition of respect for government. But utter disregard for government policy destroys the basis upon which sovereignty and central power rest. "Solidarity" strikes demonstrate how leagues of collectivities (which act like sovereignties) seeking greater autonomy are rising up against the sovereignty of central authority. Even events which are of little real importance can stimulate greater union resistance against the government.[14]

In France, during February 1920, an employee of the Society Paris-Lyon-Mediterranean was suspended for two days for having left work without permission. Although this suspension was in accordance with railroad regulations, it was sufficient provocation for unions to declare a general strike. In similar cases, attempts to convince people to follow laws and regulations have been labelled "violations of union freedom." It is actually similar to a violation of medieval immunity.

There has been hesitance to limit union privileges. At the same time, union immunity has been extended to struggles between union members and non-members. If central power intervenes, the unions threaten to strike.

Under the feudal order a vassal could not entirely avoid the king's justice. The feudal hierarchy led directly to the king. A lord could not refuse to administer the law and could not subvert the justice dispensed by a superior lord. Perhaps an analogous guarantee will one day be present in union law, but for the present it is lacking.

Most people fail to recognize that anarchy is on the ascent, although it has already manifested itself in a variety of ways. If present trends continue, struggles among the various unions will grow in frequency and importance. Hence, there will not only be conflict between unions on one side and the rest of the population on the other side, but there will also be conflict among the various unions.[15]

An analogous phenomenon was observed during the Middle Ages. Conflicts developed among those who sought to divide the spoils of central power. As long as central power remains strong, its competitors are united, or divisiveness is at least reduced by their common interests. Under the Carolingians, the great esquires sought above all else to escape supervision by imperial or royal power. For the moment our unions seek to free themselves from the prevailing power of Parliamentary authority and the interests of the rest of the population. On January 27, 1920, in a meeting of the International Office

The Crumbling of Central Authority   47

of Labor, Mr. Guerin asserted that Parliamentary authority was intact, but Mr. Jouhaut retorted that the government's only role was ratification of policies set by the International Organization of Labor as a superordinate economic parliament.[16]

As central power weakens, rivalries among its adversaries grow more apparent. Private wars of Capetian feudal factions appeared in the Middle Ages, and conflicts of the same kind can be expected to develop among unions. We already see signs of such armed conflicts between organized labor and scabs, between reds and strikebreakers, between reds and whites. In the same way that kings once failed to intervene in wars between barons, the government fails to intervene in conflict between labor factions such as Ghibellines and Guelphs.

In Padua, on April 18, 1920, reds and whites fought in dei Signori Square. This was a serious battle involving about five thousand people on each side, and fifteen people were wounded. The government failed to intervene. It watched with the same kind of inaction which characterized the response of weak kings to conflict among strong nobles.

Railroad workers, seamen, dock workers, and miners are the leading edges of the union movement and the amorphous mass comprising the rest of society. The most powerful and audacious unions overwhelm weaker and more cautious people. In England they comprise the triple alliance of miners, railroad workers, and dock workers. In France it is the General Labor Federation. As always in such cases, an "elite" dominates while the majority of the people remain unaware or unconcerned. But a weak sense of resistance is already starting to build among the majority. It could disappear momentarily, but it will surely continue to reappear and grow stronger in the more distant future.

Conflict is developing between peasants on one side and workers and government employees on the other side. This conflict is apparent in France and Italy. The form this conflict will ultimately take remains uncertain, but it will have consequences for future inter-union rivalry.

It is useful for those who dominate society to hide the fact that their privileges burden the rest of the population. They find complacent flatterers who claim that the rich carry the burden of society. But in the end the facts disclose this to be false. At any rate, if we ignore such theories, it becomes clear that those who pay for the privileges of the rich eventually rebel. They will not be restrained by honeyed words or the mawkish lectures of slovenly talkers. Such talkers profess Tolstoyan theories, knowingly or unknowingly, and encourage people to resign themselves to the "inevitable," to believe in the "divinity" of workers, to "transform themselves in order to avoid destruction." This actually means killing oneself in order to avoid being killed.

All this can have some effect on the cowardly and idiotic bourgeoisie. The bourgeoisie is as degenerate as any elite in a state of decay. However, such theories have little effect on energetic members of the new elite. These include, for example, the followers of someone like Lenin.

Once conflicts between unions and the other elements of society increase in frequency, it will be necessary to move toward some resolution. Resolution will be necessary if one does not want society to shatter and to be reduced to a state of anarchy. But it is useless to try to resolve such conflicts now because effective resolutions are to be found in practice rather than in theory. In England the theory of parliamentary government developed after rather than before parliamentary practice, and the theory was modified over time in accordance with changes in the political system. Similarly, no theory guided transformation of the government of Charles Albert of Savoy into the contemporary Italian government. This transformation was the result of practical acts whose results could not have been easily predicted.

There is no reason to believe that the general pattern of future events will differ substantially from the general pattern of past events. For this reason, one can confidently say that government via unions would not eradicate the problems and tensions that have emerged under parliamentary government. Change in form of government does not provide the substance for a solution.

Theories suggesting that parliamentary bodies are microcosms of nation-states are false. In reality parliaments represent only the dominant strata of society. The upper strata can dominate through cunning or by making promises to the masses. The maxim, inherited from previous epochs, upon which parliamentary government was founded, is that people who pay taxes are entitled to approve them. Implicitly or explicitly, there is now a new maxim. It is that those who do not pay taxes are allowed to impose taxes on others. Once servants could be "cut to pity and mercy." Today this can be done to the well-to-do. Once servants had to bare the cost of a lord's warlike madness. Today some of the wealthy must make up for the warlike madness of others. Once the emigration of labor was severly restricted. Now the movement of capital is forbidden. Small oscillations like those noted above are occurring right now. Before World War I the Italian government protected capitalist interests by erecting obstacles to labor migration. Today the government protects the interests of workers by erecting obstacles to prevent the movement of capital. Depretis sent soldiers to harvest the crops of landowners engaged in disputes with workers. The government now aids the strikers in such conflicts, even when supporting those strikers means allowing crops to rot in the fields. But theory and legislation have not changed to reflect the new reality. University students are exposed to the same theories that were taught at the time of Depretis. It would be futile to search through legal codes for a legislative act sanctioning this change in practice.

A recent article by Rigola is a sign of the contrast between present law and the code that will perhaps replace it:

> The Mazzoni case . . . represents a new phase in the struggle between capital and labor in Italy. . . . The Textile Federation ordered the Mazzoni firm, which owns half a dozen factories spread throughout Piedmont in northern Italy, to

The Crumbling of Central Authority   49

> accept standards for wages and working conditions adopted by the Cotton Association, an association of manufacturers to which the Mazzoni firm did not belong.[17]

At present the old code is only an irritant to powerful groups. Perhaps laws in the future will give workers the right to impose such requirements on corporations. However, workers have no such right under current law.

> The Mazzoni brothers resisted the request. . . . Several days went by without resolution of the conflict being reached, and workers grew exasperated by the stubbornness of their employers. The Prefect of Turin offered to mediate but the Mazzoni brothers refused to negotiate. They were then held in contempt, and workers at the Pont Canavese and Torre Pellice plants took advantage of the situation to seize control of their factories. The red flags were raised and production was organized along communistic lines.[18]

The Mazzoni brothers were guilty of committing heresy against an emerging religion. Future legislation is unlikely to tolerate such intransigence on the part of employers.

Are such actions lawful? Who cares about the law? The workers certainly do not. They are already trying to apply legal codes which have not yet developed. The central government does not care either. Its only concern is to avoid being devoured by a beast it cannot control.

Were the barons' usurpations lawful at the beginning of the feudal period? Who cared about such usurpations? The barons certainly did not. Their force of arms was enough to replace existing law. The king lacked the strength to make barons obey him.

Deciding who should control factories is more than a legal matter. It is also an economic matter. Different sets of issues must be discussed as a result. One has to pay attention to the problem of acquiring new factories as well as consider rights of ownership over existing plants. Governments that take existing plants away from owners run the risk of discouraging investment in new facilities. Added measures would then have to be taken in order to insure economic expansion.

Rigola's analysis continues. He is evenhanded and recognizes that workers acted unlawfully:

> It is true that there are no laws obliging industrialists to recognize unions or to accept government arbitration of labor disputes. It addition, it is doubtful whether refusal to accept the judgement of the Commission justifies, under current law, measures taken by the Prefect. Jurists will dispute this issue. We will simply note that the Prefect, having considered the inflexible behavior of the firm, ordered requisition of factories and gave managerial control to the Turin Section of the Department of Labor. The order notes that the Department of Labor is charged with management of the factories on behalf of the Mazzoni firm.[19]

What would happen if the same legal precedent were extended to other cases?

Consider theft of the watch of a wayfarer. The Prefect would requisition the watch and extend legal guardianship to a government ministry. The ministry would leave the watch under the temporary management of the thief.

Requisition was cancelled on April 14 after the Mazzoni brothers submitted to union demands. The government had not intervened to insure obedience to the law. On the contrary, government intervention allowed infringement of existing law. It is in this way that a government participates in the destruction of its own supremacy.

It is difficult for a civilized people to survive without laws. Laws can be written, determined by practice, or created by some other means, but laws inevitably develop because every state of affairs gives rise to its own theory. Our present state is therefore only transitory. Old laws are soon to be replaced by the new body of codes currently taking shape. If unions reign supreme, the law of the land will be union law resembling feudal law, and we will have documents similar to *The Assize of Jerusalem*. This is what union men hope for, and it is what their shy adversaries dread.

Evolution will not stop there. The ascendance of force always fosters growing contrasts. In the Middle Ages sanctuaries for persecuted servants rose and flourished. In the future analogous sanctuaries for oppressed capitalists may be established.

Feudal lords eventually discovered that their profit was never maximized by impoverishing their servants. This discovery was efficaciously put into practice by kings and was the source of their widening authority. People in our society will eventually realize that the collective good is damaged when savers are ruined, or even only discouraged. However, it may actually take a long time for this to be recognized because our society has a great deal of capital to squander. Those who wake up to this realization will be swayed by self-interest rather than anti-capitalist rhetoric, just as those who have bee hives understand that taking all the honey away from the bees and letting them starve is not in the best interest of the beekeeper. They are not being "humanitarian" when they provide some support for these little animals. Instead, they are attempting to maximize their own gain. It seems that something analogous is happening in Russia under Bolshevik rule.

Many governments have been weakened or destroyed by their inability to raise needed cash. The English Commons and the Estates-General in France were convened by sovereigns in need of financial resources. Sovereigns were in need principally because of war, pensions, and in modern times, public debt. Had they had the force and will to cut expenses, they could have avoided that need and the dependency which resulted from it. Even when partially bankrupt, strong governments can continue to operate. The French monarchy under the rule of Louis XIV and Louis XV stands as an example. But Louis XVI lacked the courage to maintain the same policy. Shyness cost him his throne and his life. He was lacking in will, and there was an even more resounding lack of power. Our own government lacks both the will and the power. It is therefore in very serious trouble that may spell its ruin. Current circumstances favor the ascendance of a new social order. Tomorrow, however, an analogous set of facts could be directed against this new order. In Russia one can already see effects of oppression of savers and disorganized production that destroys wealth. In a more or less short period of time similar effects will be visible in wealthier countries.

Plutocratic interests are powerful forces operating in support of central power. State religion with its myths and its theology can be viewed from a practical or from an ideal vantage point. Each is reflected in a different set of political parties. These include nationalists or imperialists, and *classical* socialists or Marxists who are opposed to "anarchy," free competition, and unionism. The power of both sets of parties has been weakened by the events of World War I. They could have benefited from the war had it stopped earlier. But carrying the war to extremes wore the parties down. In addition, socialists were weakened ideologically by the ties they established with "democrats" for ephemeral practical advantages. In cooperating with the parties in power under the pretext of patriotism, the socialists showed support for bourgeois governments as well as for the war.

If such parties do nothing to promote the power of central government now, centripetal movement will occur in the future. Then the action of such parties, or more accurately the successors to such parties, will be efficacious and striking.

A similar undulating succession of facts was observed when feudalism rose and then declined. For instance, the repute of Marxist idealism is now in decline. This resembles what happened to the doctrine of imperialism after the death of Charlemagne. The overshadowing of the First and Second International by the Third is similar to the overshadowing of Charlemagne's imperialism by feudalism. But just as imperialism rose again in the form of royal authority, classical socialism could rise in another form to overshadow contemporary unionism.

The Catholic faith helped to promote the doctrine of royal authority. In a corresponding way, the humanitarian faith helped to promote socialism and may also be used by the party into which the socialists are transformed. Assessment of the political and social works of the Church during the Middle Ages must not be based on Church theology, the derivations of orthodoxy, on heresy, or even on the morals of prelates. Judgment regarding classical socialism must not be based on theories or on our lust for social democracy. A faith must be distinguished from its devotees. Besides, in terms of derivations there is little difference between the mystery of Holy Trinity and Marx's theory of surplus value. Each harbors hate toward some great enemy of humanity: the devil or capitalism. In substance, the medieval theocracy aimed not to destroy central power but to take possession of it. As a matter of fact, it unknowingly promoted the interests of central power. Classical socialism also aims to take possession of central power and use it for the purpose of reorganizing economic life. Classical socialism derides the "anarchy of capitalist production," but it does not seem to me that unionized production is very different.

Let us posit, as an absurd hypothesis, the childish concept that only manual labor is necessary in the production process. If people actually acted on this premise, the consequences would be opposite of those intended by the enemies of the intelligencia and adorers of the Holy Proletariat. The rarer intellectuals are, the more valued, useful, indispensable, and powerful they become. This was the main reason that prelates were powerful during the Middle Ages. Gentlemen, the worthy forerunners of those who now show disdain for intellectual activity, were proud of being illiterate. Church power declined only after the number of educated laymen increased. This was particularly the case once it was widely realized that there is more to culture than religion. Church theology of the Middle Ages was not unlike modern proletarian theology.

But we are now approaching the border between what is probable and what is merely possible. Let us be careful not to cross this boundary. Let us also avoid the danger of moving beyond the fields of possibility and roaming into the boundless spaces of imagination.

Notes

This paper was originally published in two parts, on May 20 and June 5, 1920, in *Rivista di Milano*.

1. In Roman law, *precarium* is the free concession of an object on the condition that it will be returned on demand by the grantor.[Ed.]
2. All quotations comments inside of brackets are those of Pareto.[Ed.]
3. Antonio Pertile, *Storia del diritto italiano*, Volume 1. [Ed.—A number of Pareto's references are incomplete and are presented as they appeared in the original manuscript.]
4. Sidney and Beatrice Webb, *The History of Trade Unionism* (New York: Longmans, Green, 1894).
5. Agostino Lanzillo, *La Disfatta del socialismo* (Florence: Libreria della Voce) pp. 270, 277.
6. *Pagine libere* (Milan, February 15, 1920), p. 2.
7. "The bourgeoisie must convince itself that it reaps the fruits of a crazy and suicidal policy perpetrated during five years of war. It lied to the people in order to encourage national 'resistance.' Resist! The bourgeoisie was under the illusion that it could obtain the support of the people and the armed forces by making chimerical promises it never intended to keep. Now it is hanging by the neck from its own lies." *Resto del Carlino* (March 7, 1920).
8. "Saracen" was a term used in reference to Muslims during the Middle Ages.[Ed.]
9. Capitulare primum anni DCCCII sive capitula data Missis Dominicis, anno secundo imperii Cap. I.
10. Capitularium Karoli Magni . . . lib. II. cap. XXVI.
11. Fustel de Coulanges, *Nouvelles Recherches sur quelques problèmes d'histoire* (Paris, 1891).
12. On another occasion Fustel de Coulanges was led by his own observations to the conclusions I have drawn regarding the relationship between thoughts and action. He discusses opposition between Austrasia and Neustria. [Austrasia was the East-

ern Territory of the Franks under the Merovingian kings. It included Belgium, Lorraine, and portions of the valley of the Rhine. Neustria was the Western Territory, extending from the Meuse River to the Loire River.] "Moreover, let us not suppose that these men draw their inspiration from a political doctrine or from a pure idea. There are interests and even desires which move each one of them." *(Les Transformations de la royauté pendant l'époque Carolingienne,* Paris, 1914). One could say the same thing about contemporary unions. If one discounts a few people with their imaginative visions, what the masses really want are high wages, short working hours, and greater dignity. They do not have the slightest conception of what the future will really bring.

13. "At Leghorn's railroad station, railway employees refused to allow the train on which the 231st infantry was traveling to pass. The government gave up and transported the soldiers to Genoa on the battleship Duilio. When they arrived, on the morning of April 10, the powerful metal workers' shop at Giano pier stopped work and asked that the soldiers not disembark. The strike spread throughout the port when the government refused to assent to this demand. A general strike was called later at the Port of Grazia." *Idea Nazionale* (April 21, 1920). The government did not dare to employ force against railway workers and arranged to transport troops to Turin via truck. Such facts mean little in themselves. However, they are useful to the degree that they indicate changes in sentiment among government officials and employees.

14. "Even the most unimportant organizers realize that threatening to go on strike is enough to achieve objectives. . . . The Ministry will make incredible concessions under the pretext of avoiding strikes. . . . This happened prior to the tramway and railway strike. Overused tactics were again employed. Mortara lavishly dispensed sixty million lire per year and the Committee for Fair Treatment awarded 140 or 150 million. People in official circles justified these expenditures by saying that circumstances required that they prevent suspension of public service." The same thing has happened in England and France at various times. "This is said as if a strike had actually been avoided. Actual observers saw events from a different vantage point when tramway employees left work in order to have their leaders announce victory. No less unedifying, railway employees left Lombardy and the entire industrial region without service. Adding insult to injury, the reason for disruption of services remains unclear."

"In the wake of dissension among ministers, there has been no decree ratifying current measures." What of Parliament? It seems to exist for the purpose of approving the dictates of unions and ministers. "Organizers are preparing to interpret these measures in a manner which suits them. Citizens and railway managers are deliberately kept in the dark about the nature of these measures." *Idea Nazionale* (February 29, 1920).

The central government is not even able to inspire sufficient obedience to operate the trains and tramways on schedule. Unions care so little for government prerogative that they simply refuse to comply with daylight savings time. Daylight savings time may be a childish measure but it does fall within the domain of government control. "If daylight savings time really does have economic advantages, why doesn't the government make people comply unconditionally? And if daylight savings time is not useful, why has it been decreed?" *Idea Nazionale* (April 16, 1920).

The answer is easy. It has been decreed by virtue of power which exists in theory but not in practice. Similar contradictions were observed when feudal lords prevailed on royal power, and more generally when local power and special interests prevail upon central power.

15. The *Conference of Simple Workers* held in London on March 11, 1920, approved a resolution. "Nowadays the worst enemies of labor are not the capitalists, but the workers' lieutenants. Consequently, the *Conference* is resolved that regulations for the society must be agreed upon throughout the United Kingdom."
16. *Comité national d'études sociales et politiques*, Vol.2, No. 12.
17. *Il Resto del Carlino* (March 18, 1920).
18. Ibid.
19. Ibid

3

The Plutocratic Cycle

Examining another aspect of the phenomenon in question will provide further insight into the underlying dynamics we seek to discover. Let us consider the patterns of economic and social development in European societies over the past century or more. A number of observations can be made if we examine long-term trends rather than incidental disturbances. First, wealth has greatly increased. And along with wealth, savings and capital invested in productive enterprise have also increased. Second, wealth continues to be unequally distributed. Although, from the vantage points of some, inequality may seem to increase or decline, the overall distribution of wealth has remained about the same. Third, two social classes have steadily gained in power and importance: the class of wealthy speculators and the class of wage earners—factory workers in particular, but more generally, all wage earners. Speaking in a rather vague and loose way, the growing power of wealthy speculators might be viewed as a "plutocratic" tendency while the growing power of wage earners might be viewed as a "democratic" tendency. Fourth, these two classes can be thought of as having in some sense cooperatively united or formed a partial alloy. This trend has been particularly apparent since the end of the nineteenth century. Even though the interests of speculators and workers do not correspond completely, it happens that certain members of both classes find it profitable to operate in the same way—to impose themselves upon the state and use it to exploit the remaining social classes. It also follows that plutocrats are able to forge an effective union because they are astute and can deceive the masses by manipulating public sentiment. This gives rise to the widely observed phenomenon of demagogic plutocracy. Fifth, while the power of speculators and wage earners is growing, the power of the two remaining classes is declining. That is to say that the class of independent property owners who are wealthy or well-to-do but do not speculate, and the military class, are losing power. In particular, the power of the military classes has markedly diminished. And although the military remained powerful in Germany until World War I, its power has now declined even in that nation. An extension of suffrage from the haves to the have-nots is one sign of the intensity of this change. It must be noted that the haves include many people who are not speculators, and the have-nots include many people who have interests in common with speculators. The have-nots also include many who can be taken advantage of because they have sentiments (and manifest behavioral residues) that can be used by speculators. This has often been done in order to augment the power of speculators at the expense of wage earners. Sixth, little by little, control over instruments of force passes from superior to inferior classes. This characteristic and the next are aspects of the shattering of central power. Seventh, modern parliaments seem to be an effective tool of demagogic plutocracy. First in elections and later during deliberations, parliamentary procedures favor those who are skilled in manipulative dealings. It is for this reason that parliamentary government follows, in part, the fate of plutocracy. It thrives and declines with plutocracy. Transformations in parliamentary order, which are also transformations in democracy, are correlated with the plutocratic cycle.

Some facts must be placed in their proper historical perspective. We must avoid the common habit of attaching excessive importance to what happens before our own eyes while disregarding the past. We must also avoid the opposite inclination of presuming that the present is a faithful and precise repetition of the past. The study of history makes it clear that passage of time is invariably characterized by cyclical oscillations rather than uniform change in a single direction. In spite of the complexities involved, we can recognize a general pattern of oscillation. This pattern arises from man's own nature. We are regulated and governed by agents divided into two groups: one preferring to rule primarily through consensus and the other preferring to rule primarily through the use of force (2251). The social order consequently fluctuates between these two poles.

Consensus can be obtained through different kinds of appeal. Consensus can be predicated upon community of interests, or upon religious sentiments, customs, prejudices, etc. The latter correspond to residues, which I identified as "persistence of aggregates" in *Treatise on General Sociology*. People motivated by customs and prejudices tend to be swayed by the persuasive efforts of persons using analytical reasoning or, as is more often the case, constructing derivations that rationalize or legitimize a particular line of conduct. These manipulative skills correspond to the "instinct of combination." It is instructive to note how major categories of citizens have participated in government. Consider the two largest categories: the first one formed by farmworkers and landowners, the other one by tradesman, industrialists, and managers of public works. "Persistence of aggregates" [or stubborn adherence to established ways] is almost always strong in the first group. "Combinations" [or deceit and cunning] are almost always strong in the second. Therefore, the character of society will differ fundamentally depending upon the category from which leadership originates. When the first category dominates, the ruling elite can support itself. But when the second category dominates, society often becomes more plutocratic. For in consuming more than it produces, such an elite will often find it advantageous to institute demagogic or military control in order to solidify its position. Demagogic control is less expensive to exercise than military control as long as the elite minimizes its warlike undertakings.

The inclination to rule through use of force and the inclination to rule by obtaining consensus often appear separately and in opposition. Exceptional individuals can have both sets of inclinations and accompanying skills, but the majority of governors tend to rely on one much more than the other. The fundamental character of the society changes cyclically as classes circulate and as one inclination replaces another.

Each of these systems of order can generate initial prosperity, but it then spawns decadence and decay. In this respect the fate of social systems is similar to the life cycle of living creatures.[1] Oscillations correspond to such periods.

A theory of undulatory change in societies can be derived from these notions, which are only a compendium of experimental facts. This theory was dealt with at great length in *Treatise on General Sociology*. Consequently, we will only recall those passages that are relevant to our present concern.

Ancient Rome was a republic of farmworkers that became a plutocracy after the destruction of Carthage and the conquest of Greece. Agrarian laws [133-121 B.C.] initiated by the Gracchi brothers were intended to prevent this transformation and hastened it instead.[2] But this is not at all unusual. On the contrary, politicians frequently seek to insure one state of affairs while unwittingly promoting the opposite. Roman demagogic plutocracy triumphed until Sulla's time [138-78 B.C., dictator 82-79 B.C.]. From that period until the time of Augustus [63 B.C.-14 A.D., effective ruler after 31 B.C.], the forces of demagogic plutocracy fought against the forces of military plutocracy. The empire eventually degenerated into a military bureaucracy similar in part to that of tsarist Russia.[3] Both periods ended in cataclysmic social change. Mario and Caesar took advantage of demagogy and unknowingly prepared for the reign of Augustus. Only history will tell if the Soviet government will be subject to analogous vicissitudes and if Ivan the Terrible will have a successor with Lenin or following Lenin.

Agricultural interests dominated during the Middle Ages. This dominance was then destroyed, little by little, by mercantile interests with the aid of royal power and bureaucracy. Several types of plutocracy appeared in the transformations leading to the modern period.

The extraordinary prosperity of the English plutocracy is notable. It is very similar to the Roman experience before the end of the republic. In both cases the principal sources of prosperity were farmers and rentiers who provided the demagogic plutocracy with elements of stability and force which it otherwise lacked.

In France Napoleon III [1808-73] moderated the growth of plutocracy, basing his reign [1852-70] on agricultural interests and making use of militarism. In this respect his reign resembled that of Augustus. Both regimes also ended with military confrontations against foreign adversaries. But the French empire was destroyed at Sedan while the Roman empire was only shaken by the defeat which Germans [led by Arminius] inflicted upon the legions of General Varus. Thus, accidental events are added to the bigger pattern of oscillations arising from intrinsic forces.

Agricultural interests were dominant at the inception of the Third French Republic; however, the republic was soon transformed into a demagogic plutocracy which reached the height of its power during the period of the "Dreyfus affair."[4] But war is not favorable to plutocracies, and the most recent elections in France indicate the possibility of an oscillation in the opposite direction. The agricultural class was enriched during World War I and has gained new importance. Small farm owners prevail in this class, and it therefore tends to have, even if only in some small degree, characteristics that are popularly called conservative. The French agricultural class lacks the kind of laborers one finds in Italy, who are paid a daily wage, ask for expropriation of lands, and even ask to be paid for useless or fictitious projects.

Frenchmen have always been warlike, and their victory in World War I has strengthened militarism considerably. The socialists have not kept faith with their principles; they have joined forces with the bourgeois government, and among them there are some insincere patriots and even some profiteers. The power and importance of socialists have diminished as a result. We do not know if this recent trend, which began with the shattering of central power, will continue. We do not know what the final outcome will be.

In Germany there was a military plutocracy aided by landed interests, especially those in Prussia. The German military plutocracy has now been destroyed by rival Western plutocracies.

Let us disregard the insincere patriot making ethical pronouncements about the "defense of right and justice," the "barbarity of the enemy," and so on. Then World War I, to a great extent, looks like a conflict between military plutocracy and demagogic plutocracy in which the Russian bureaucracy intervened. In this sense the socialist analysis of World War I is correct. It was a bourgeois war.

Ruling elites, except for those in America and perhaps in England, miscalculated. Given the unrest that followed in the aftermath of the Russo-Japanese War, the Russian government should have foreseen the revolution [of 1917] but it ignored the warnings. The German government should have learned from Bismarck that the road to war must be prepared through diplomacy. But it was presumptuous and did not care to learn. And the French and especially the Italian plutocracies failed to prepare for war even as they were moving toward it.

Leaders of the plutocracies initially believed that World War I would be short and inexpensive. And later, when they knew the truth, they wanted to continue making common people believe that costs associated with the war would be limited.[5] World War I could have been very useful for the plutocrats because the art of governing resides in knowing how to take advantage of existing sentiments (2247 et passim), and patriotic sentiments were very strong. But plutocracies did not know how to stop in time, which is a common defect of such enterprises. They could have made peace in 1917 at a point when the war would have been useful rather than damaging to them.[6] On the contrary, countries of the Entente [France, England, Russia, and later Italy] wanted to win, while the side of the Central Empires [Germany, Austria-Hungary, and Turkey] could not be resigned to the inevitable sacrifices required if one is to minimize losses by admitting defeat. Now both sides face almost insolvable problems. In this way the process of unfolding events, a process that perhaps would have occurred anyway, was quickened.

The Western plutocratic classes failed to realize that German and Russian militarism were indirectly useful. Not even the so-called conservatives (although it is unclear why they are called conservatives) realized this. Nor did the plutocratic classes realize that they gave the opposing demagogy a free hand by destroying German militarism, after the tsarist government had already disappeared. Now they want to act by fighting against Bolshevism, but it is too late. The Russian revolutionaries have allies inside the other nations of the Entente, allies which are powerful and dangerous. And the more powerful they grow, the more that centralized authority will shatter. Supporters of centralized power try to maintain their positions by dint of expedients. In part, plutocrats allowed themselves to be misled by the same derivations they once used to deceive others and to induce the masses to stay in the trenches, adding to these derivations excessive promises they knew they could not keep.[7] One can really say in this case that the snake bit the swindler. A person who is sly is eventually deceived by someone even more cunning.

The military plutocracy in Germany was defeated by a foreign force. That was the demagogic plutocracy that is now spreading into Germany and has completely triumphed in the countries of the Entente.

Modern Italy was constituted by the bourgeoisie with indifference and sometimes opposition from the rural multitudes.[8] The new government soon turned to demagogic plutocracy, which reached the peak of its power with Depretis and just afterward. As usual, the demagogic plutocracy has been damaged by the war, but it has not been defeated.

Generally speaking, the demagogic plutocracy now seems to be entirely triumphant. Perhaps it will be able to maintain itself for a long time in England, supported by earnings gained through the colonial hegemony which all powerful nations except the United States have pursued, willy-nilly. Rome exploited only the Mediterranean basin. England exploits a large part of the terrestrial globe. Only the future can tell whether effective internal forces will arise against the demagogic plutocracy in England, whether military plutocracy will arise again in other countries, and what uncertainties are in store in Russia and Asia.

Plutocracy is in greater danger in other European countries. But regardless of the time or place, we find plutocracy capable of turning desperate conditions to its own advantage. It apparently yields to rival forces with wily plans devised for recouping losses and concessions made to strong opponents. It circumvents obstacles it cannot overcome directly. And as usual, those people who are productive and delay gratification pay the costs of such conflict. They are all like good lambs, ready to be sheared.

The plutocracy has invented countless makeshift programs, such as generating enormous public debt that plutocrats know they will never be able to repay, levies on capital, taxes which exhaust the incomes of those who do not speculate, sumptuary laws which have historically proven useless, and other similar measures. The principal goal of each of these measures is to deceive the multitudes.

In Italy the Honorable Member of Parliament Falcioni's bill concerning "latifundium and concessions of lands to peasants" will not reduce contemporary plutocracy any more than the Gracchi agrarian laws harmed the plutocratic classes in Rome after a short period of tumultuous adjustment.[9] If it were effective it could damage the plutocracy, as could the "Popolari" bill to increase the number of small landowners, because such an agricultural class is now the only rival plutocratic interests have to fear.

Bread sold below cost of production, housing sold at reduced price, and other benefits are provided citizens. But as long as the production of savings is not too damaged, plutocratic interests will be able to continue enriching themselves in the same way that enrichment occurred during the Roman plutocracy. Food rationing acts were initiated during the republican period and then retained and expanded by the empire.

Such similarities in general conditions and responses are inherent in the very nature of the plutocratic cycle. Therefore, present trends will continue for a time, and the decadence of Roman plutocracy could really be, at least to some extent, the image of plutocracy which is our impending fate.

Certainly, we are now [1920] at a point that is analogous to the one in which the Roman plutocracy found itself at the end of the republic. Also, if we are to consider analysis of cycles in different countries and at different points in time, it seems very likely that, being close to the peak of a cycle, we are soon to embark upon a descent.

This analysis has been brief, and one would like to know more. But it is better to know a little than to know nothing at all. For knowing a little does not exclude the possibility of acquiring deeper understanding. On the contrary, knowing a little prepares the road for learning more in the future. If we are to learn more, experimental science must be our trustworthy guide.

Notes

This chapter was originally published on July 5, 1920, in *Rivista di Milano*.
1. See *Treatise on General Sociology* (2541).
2. Tiberius Sempronius Gracchus and Caius Sempronius Gracchus, sons of Cornelia, were Roman statesmen and reformers. Tiberius was alarmed by the great inequities of his time, and stood for tribunate in 133 B.C. He immediately passed the Sempronian (agrarian reform) Law and was murdered in the same year. Caius tried to complete his brother's work, and initiated a number of important social reforms prior to his death in a riot in 121 B.C. But the ruling class opposed these reforms in letter as well as in spirit, and successfully subverted their operation.[Ed.]
3. This will not be expanded upon here because it is described in great detail in *Treatise on General Sociology*. Although *Treatise* was written before World War I, modern plutocracies have precisely the characteristics described in that work. Similarly, contemporary events confirm our earlier forecasts of cyclical change.
4. Captain Alfred Dreyfus (1859-1935) of the French army, a Jewish Alsatian, was convicted in 1894 of selling military secrets to the Germans. Dreyfus was convicted on slim evidence and never stopped protesting his innocence. The government suppressed evidence of another person's possible guilt, and when that evidence was finally made public the Dreyfus case became a major political issue. It remained an issue for over a decade.[Ed.]
5. When leaders were trying to convince people that the war would be short, I wrote: "It is likely that the present war will be a long one. One can see what a serious mistake was made by those who asserted that war had been made impossible by increased destructive power, and one will see that an equally serious mistake is being made by those who believe that the present war will not last because financial difficulties and famine will affect one or more of the belligerents." *Giornale d'Italia* (September 25, 1914). That future tense "one will see" in 1914, today, in 1920, has become the present tense "one sees," and also the past tense "one saw."
6. I wrote about this at greater length in an article titled "After Four Years of War" appearing in the journal *Coenobium* edited by Enrico Bignami. This article might not have been published elsewhere, and Mr. Bignami is to be praised for his impartiality. At the time I wrote that article I had come under attack for maintaining that the lessons of history allowed us to forecast that the League of Nations, despite appearances to the contrary, would prove to be an instrument used by powerful nations to maintain their hegemony. In which direction have things gone, and in what direction are things going? In the *Coenobium* article I repeated the forecast that many states would pay their debts by devaluing their currency. Examine the present value in gold of the monetary units of Austria, Germany, France, Italy, etc. Then assess whether states repay debts and interest with good currency or depreciated currency.
7. Now that plutocracy renews its deceit, making common people believe that, through a presumed reduction in the luxury of the well-to-do, the government will be able to pay war expenses and promote higher wages and greater employment without affecting the amount of capital investment. In this way the wasteful squandering of the war is offset not by more work and increased production but by reductions in both. Quickly note that for the moment luxury has not diminished. Instead, it seems to have moved from the old rich to the new rich, from savers to speculators. There are always people who can be taken in. Humans shall be a race of dupes for time immemorial.
8. Note that in southern provinces the opposition of the common people to bourgeoisie, the "gentlemen," was violent in 1860 and for a few years thereafter. Under the

dominion of plutocracy this opposition more or less resigned itself, but is now being rekindled and expresses itself in milder form in Popolari (or Cattolici Popolari, a political party supporting agrarian reform). Clearly, there is a tendency for forces which are repressed by central power to reappear as soon as that power weakens. This phenomenon is of great importance and is very widespread, being evidenced far beyond the boundaries of parliamentary disputes and manipulations.

9. Latifundia are large landed estates with labor in a state of semi-servitude.[Ed.]

4

Sentiments

In the previous chapter we examined the indirect manifestations of sentiments in a single case. We now turn our attention to discussion of sentiments in their own right, because sentiments are the most important determinants of social phenomena.

Sentiments cannot be directly detected. Opinions and actions are the empirical manifestations of sentiments, and only these manifestations can be directly observed.[1] Such behavioral manifestations should be studied quantitatively, rather than focusing qualitatively on any single manifestation. Of course, it is true that the opinion of a single person can be important in the physical sciences. In gravitational astronomy the opinions of Newton were worth more than the opinions of millions of his contemporaries in England. However, it is the aggregation of public sentiments, rather than the opinions of any single individual, which influence social and economic events in a nation. Social equilibrium responds to aggregate shifts in sentiment which can only be studied quantitatively.

Even a very superficial view of present society reveals streams of opinion that manifest underlying patterns in sentiments and interests. These underlying sentiments and interests [rather than opinions about specific issues] are the forces at work determining the character of social equilibrium. We must therefore avoid becoming overly preoccupied with exactly what people say, at the expense of our interest in the underlying sentiments which those indicators reflect. And because we are interested in aggregate patterns of sentiment, we should avoid preoccupation with highly unusual outlying cases.

Deeply held sentiments can assume religious form, while sentiments to which people are less fully committed sometimes manifest themselves in the expression of metaphysical or pseudo-logical opinions. Common to each is the desire people have to feel that they know what is absolutely true and scientifically unshakable. People who subscribe to some set of religious or metaphysical beliefs are able to avoid the rigors of scientific study. A priori ethical, metaphysical, or theological principles allow them to make unequivocal judgments regarding all social events. Cries for action "in defense of law and justice" fall into this category.[2] Some people take advantage of this adage. For instance, Muslims regard themselves the sole followers of the one true faith, and they believe that God allowed them to conquer large areas in order to propagate their religion. Of course, they find it more difficult to explain loss of territory. Other examples are to be found in the decline of democratic ideology, which once had so many adherents, and in the rise of proletarian ideology, which now has so many followers. Some of these followers act in good faith, while others do not. In the face of intelligent opposition, they repeat the same anathemas that the first Christians cried against pagan literature and science.

Turning to other examples of the importance of sentiment, patriotism has often armed neighboring cities against one another. Sparta was armed against Athens. Florence was armed against Pisa. Centuries later patriotic cause pushed whole "nations" into war and imperial adventure. As a final example, sacrosanct humanitarianism manifested itself as patriotism in the oratory of Isocrates in Athens [436-338 B.C.]. It was later to shed its terrestrial veil as Beatrice did with Dante. Humanitarianism also manifests itself in programs for universal peace such as that of Kant. There have been many such programs but they have never been successful. We now see yet another such attempt in formation of the League of Nations.

We should act as outside observers when we examine people's opinions and actions. We should not praise or decry those beliefs, nor should we support or libel, propagate or extinguish them. We merely accept their presence as fact and attempt to find relationships between one set of manifestations and another.

In every religion, levels of faith and commitment differ from one person to another. Expressions of faith can be sincere and fervent, moderately strong, rather poor and somewhat skeptical, mere pretense, completely absent, or clearly hypocritical.

Those who make sentimental judgments tend to assume that a religion embraced by hypocrites is a weak religion. But for those who reason experimentally, hypocrisy is a sign of the power of a faith, because people only pretend to be things which are well accepted by others. In this respect Giovanni Boccaccio's [1313-1375] tale contains an important element of truth. He relates the story of an Israelite who became a Catholic after observing that Catholics were not convinced to renounce their beliefs by the cruel and wicked ways of Roman prelates. Nowadays, a sure sign of the power of democratic ideology is the fact that so many people pretend to accept it. A sure sign of the decadence of aristocratic ideology is that it has no hypocritical pretenders at all. Similarly, observers have long noted that heresies appear when a religion is prosperous and flourishing, and disappear when the religion is in decay.

We must not be swayed by censorship, which is too easily arrived at. Rather, we should be practical and recognize that religion provides jobs through which many people support themselves and pursue riches, honor, and power. But hypocrisy on the part of church bureaucrats does not prove the religion to be weak. Similarly, noisy patriotism was to the advantage of those plutocrats who grew rich as a result of the war. But many others were moved by pure ideals and risked their lives and property in performance of heroic acts. The number of people motivated by ideals is not small in comparison with the number of people motivated by self-interest. Therefore, we should assess the magnitude of streams of opinion. This may require that we disregard some accidents and artifices in favor of quantitative examination of aggregate patterns.

In every society one can observe contrasts among the social classes.[3] Displays of sentiment follow the general law of rhythm. They increase and then they diminish. The present oscillation has the following characteristics. Among workers (or proletarians if one prefers that term) displays of hatred against those who are wealthy and cultured are growing in intensity. Bolsheviks epitomize this, but such sentiments are remarkably strong the world over. On the opposite side, upper-class displays of hatred for workers have disappeared. In many cases the well-to-do flatter workers in a manner akin to the way in which they once flattered royalty. Workers sound their trumpets and prepare for the attack, while the well-to-do bow their heads in capitulation or sell their own class for thirty pieces of silver by siding with the masses. But let us keep our objective in sight. We must uncover the relationship between these manifestations and the sentiments they represent.

Manifestations of class hostility emanating from the proletariat may reflect a recent relaxation in social control. In the past workers were restrained from displaying such feelings, and when restrictions were relaxed, there was a natural outpouring of emotion. But even if we take this into consideration, the class antagonism is unmistakable. This becomes apparent when one examines concrete cases. Compare the sentiments of a sharecropper toward a landowner in Tuscany today with those which prevailed fifty years ago. Or compare the sentiments of a petty bureaucrat toward the state today with those of a civil servant in some prior era.

Indeed, the famous comedy *The Miseries of Travet* now seems archaic.[4] Attitudes have changed among citizens from all walks of life. It was once thought that the attitudes of industrial workers changed because of the transformation from small-scale production to economic dominance by large firms. But attitudes have changed among workers in all sectors of the economy, including those sectors which have remained relatively unaffected by modernization. Consequently, mode and scale of production can explain only some of the attitudinal changes observed in the population at large. There has been a general shift in attitudes of the working class. They are, to use the modern jargon, more "conscious" and "progressive."

Many people in the upper class are "progressive" as well. But this "progressivism" is ironically different from that of the working class. Many well-to-do have lost heart and patiently suffer every insult, menace, and oppression. They humbly submit to their opponents, kissing the very hands that despoil them. They rely on sly manners to achieve goals, rather than upon courage and force.

During strikes wealthy people enlist the aid of scabs by making promises they never intend to keep. Then in the aftermath of the strikes, they cowardly abandon the scabs to the anger of strikers. Even if capitalists win, they are afraid to act decisively and as a consequence make concessions in order to "pacify the hearts" of workers. Because the workers never lose under this scenario, "pacification" actually encourages further conflict.

Sentiments of personal defense and property are weakening among the wealthy. The "social function" of property has come to be precariously defined in terms of "social obligation," while work has been transformed into a "right." For example, in some parts of Italy workers invade agricultural lands and arbitrarily perform unnecessary tasks, saying that they have a right to work, and that landowners have a corresponding obligation to pay peasants for whatever work they choose to perform. Many well-to-do approve of this state of affairs.

Aristotle describes the oligarchs of his time by noting that "in some cities they take an oath 'to be enemies of the people and harm the people as much as possible.' They should instead adopt the opposite attitude and swear 'not to wrong the people.'"[5] Aristotle's admonition was taken to heart by some people throughout the nineteenth and early twentieth centuries. Many rich people actually believe that they are keeping faith with Aristotle's call for benevolent rule. But others, especially plutocrats, merely pretend to believe in the benevolence of their leadership.

When the Estates-General were convened in France in 1614, the Third Estate wished to improve upon its inferior position relative to the clergy and nobility. Members of the nobility were angered by such impudence and Baron Senecey stated their case in an audience with the king. "I am ashamed, Sire, to have to inform you of the terms which once again have offended us. The Third Estate affirms the ecclesiastical order to be the oldest, ours younger than the ecclesiastical, and theirs the youngest. They say it often comes to pass that houses ruined by the elders are rebuilt by the youngest. . . . Not satisfied to call themselves our brothers, they usurp the restoration of the State."[6] Nowadays the terms are exactly reversed. Workers get annoyed when they are compared with capitalists rather than the other way around. This is true in the Soviet Union and elsewhere as well.

The endless disagreements between medieval Italian republics are well known and do not need explication. Although some fraud and deception were known at the time, courage and strength grew radiant in those republics. This was true among common people as well as among the nobility. But many clear examples of oscillation occurred in important respects. Muratori describes life in the city:

> Noblemen aspiring to public office and honors often found it necessary to unlawfully join the gilds in order to achieve their goals. Once in the company of gildmen, nobles became eligible for more offices. They succeeded in controlling the plebes [just as our twentieth century plutocrats control workers] because their very presence demonstrated valued esteem. Perhaps today's [1790] nobles would be ashamed to yield so much, but noblemen of old were not so delicate. They were willing to yield in order to promote their own advancement.[7]

Now [1920] we find ourselves returning once again to times like those described by Muratori. When a new elite gains power, it is conceivable that they will act like the elite Muratori describes.

There have also been important changes in sentiments concerning taxation. It was once considered fair for the tax burden to fall squarely on the poor while the wealthy escaped taxation. Now the terms have been reversed. This demonstrates, by the way, just how "fair" the scales of justice are. Lady justice never fails to deny her assistance to the most powerful. Systems in which taxpayers approve of taxes were once thought of as free.[8] Taxes are now imposed by those who are, for all intents and purposes, exempt from paying those taxes. It is popular to refer to such a tax system as free. This demonstrates that "free" can mean as many different things as the term "fair" can mean.

It is remarkable that opposite sentiments can express themselves in the same terms. In the past, people accepted the principle of taxation but opposed taxes that were burdensome. Nowadays, the well-to-do accept the very principles of taxation that impoverish them. They never unite in order to reject taxes. Instead, they content themselves with partial escape by finding tax shelters and loopholes. This places the burden of the tax load on their neighbors. The well-to-do are ever weaker because of this internal discord, for governments always follow the path of least resistance. In the past, governments taxed the common people because they were disorganized and powerless. Now, the well-to-do are taxed because they are unorganized.

In 1715, finances of the French monarchy were in disarray, similar to the current condition of many nations. The Duke of Saint-Simon refused to accept the presidency of the Council of Finances, and his justification (pp. 401, 404-5) is instructive:

> I see only two options. We can continue to augment taxes in order to reduce the immense debt, eventually crushing everyone under the tax burden. Or we can declare public bankruptcy by announcing that the future king will not be encumbered by any of the debts of the present king, his grandfather and predecessor. This would be an enormous injustice and would ruin a great number of families. [In spite of the costs involved, Saint-Simon prefers this measure as the least harmful.] The louder the cries of despair about disorder and difficulty in the lives of so many private individuals, the more cautious and wise that private citizens will be in the future. This will have two marvelous consequences. First, the king will be less capable of obtaining immense sums for the indulgence of his personal pleasures. . . . This will encourage wisdom and moderation in

68   The Transformation of Democracy

> his reign, rather than brigandage and perpetual war. . . . Second, France will be delivered from the people who are its real enemies. Those enemies are bent on devouring her resources by every invention that avarice can imagine, and they have developed a fatal science. The administration and collection of diverse taxes are more deadly than the tax rates themselves. Many privileged people, deprived of all useful social functions, now contribute to the destruction of society by pillaging private enterprise, interrupting commerce of all kinds, and using the law to shackle and control the actions of productive members of society.[9]

This description is universal in its application to different historical periods.

Yet another parallel can be drawn to contemporary events. The ease with which taxes could be raised and debts incurred at the time was a factor leading to the ruin of the French monarchy. Raising money via the progressive income tax and by incurring government debt are now so widespread that the art of government seems to be summarized in such devices. This may have some bearing on the ruin which menaces the bourgeois state.[10]

Western governments have risked financial collapse in order to pay debts with depreciated currency. But, it would be difficult to find members of the bourgeoisie with ideas like those of Saint-Simon. The absence of such expression reflects the prejudices and timid habits of the well-to-do, rather than any exasperation over the futility of expressing that point of view or revulsion over the fact that government revenues support enemies of the capitalist class.

Capitalists find many ways of excusing and justifying their actions. The nucleus of these excuses is: "We have been forced to make war in order to defend ourselves. We must now retire debts incurred during the war and this requires that everyone make sacrifices."

This reasoning is predicated on sentiment rather than logic. If people tried to follow it, they would discover that both sides in any conflict justify their actions in the name of defense. But it is difficult to understand how two rival factions can be forced to mount a horrendous defense when no faction is on the offense. We would observe that attaching the label of "defense" to plans for dominating the terrestrial globe is certainly stretching the truth. And refusing to accept past losses in order to obtain peace is equally absurd. Prolongation of the war, and most of the expense associated with the war, resulted from just such plans and intentions.

It is not true that economies were ruined exclusively by the expense of war. Other government policies are largely responsible for current difficulties. Politicians eager to gain supporters and soothe opponents are all too willing to waste money by extending benefits, subsidizing prices, engaging in unnecessary public works, militarizing, and tolerating disorder. Economies are also ruined by citizens, often with the complicity of governments. People get lazy and insubordinate, and they make excessive requests that cannot be satisfied. The nouveaux riches also waste resources by living in ostentatious luxury. That was tolerated during the war because their support was needed.

They behave exactly like Trimalcione.[11] But, at least Trimalcione made his riches by profiting from trade rather than war, and enjoyed those riches in a time of abundance rather than a time of general famine. Production of consumable goods and services declined during World War I. But everyone always wants to consume more. Is this possible?

The rich delude themselves with daydreams about increased wealth, yet to be realized from war production.[12] The well-to-do are also daydreaming when they think that sumptuary laws will moderate consumption. In truth, such measures seem as inefficacious now as they ever were in the past.

The poor try to avoid the issue by transforming it into a moral question. They ask what conditions should exist rather than what conditions are practical to expect. People say that the present increase in consumption by the poor can be compensated for by reduced consumption by the rich. But this is erroneous because a small decline in consumption cannot compensate for a big increase.

Subsidies for the price of bread encourage consumption. Unemployment benefits encourage idleness among those who would prefer not to accept low wages. Better wages are being offered to factory workers, wage earners, and craftsmen for less work than they once performed. Transportation systems are stagnating, and the problem is exasperated by enormous wages, the eight-hour working day, laziness, carelessness, and the strange pretenses of civil servants who forget they are employees. Profiteering sharks squander resources. Speculation replaces production. One might ask what all these things have to do with war.

All these things are, in part, an indirect consequence of war, reflecting changes in sentiment and artifices of government that have their origins in war. But on the other hand, those people whose sentiments and interests produce these trends cannot exculpate themselves by ascribing the effects to the war.

It is amusing to say that *everyone* must bear the sacrifices of war when you see that the people who work the least also earn the most, while other people are deprived of everything they have. Moreover, instead of representing the interests of everyone, the state is the instrument of the dominant class. One could say that it is now the proletarians who are in charge, but in truth the state is controlled by those who are devious enough to capture its helm. This is nothing new.

Governments spend a portion of their budgets for servicing loans. And since interest is being paid, there must also be someone who benefits. It is therefore necessary to interpret pleas for deficit spending with a grain of salt in order to uncover the real reasons one supports such policies. Of course, it would be a mistake to believe that all the preachers, or even most of them, are motivated by pecuniary interest. But they yield to sentiments, and many are effective apostles.

The fact that government departments have continued to dictate policy even after the war might suggest to some that popular sentiments favor greater centralization of power. But history belies such an induction and shows that governments turn to absolutism at the same time that they grow weak.[13] Politicians understand that opposition can actually strengthen a regime.

From this line of argument it can be deduced that, because of their respective sentiments, today's working-class people are more forceful and concerted than the well-to-do. The common people are at present more firmly united, more loyal, more brave, more energetic, more willing to defend their ideals, more wise, more constant, and more goal-directed than the well-to-do. Workers are less cunning than the well-to-do, but in periods of turmoil their forcefulness will compensate for this shortcoming.

People with sentiments that are forceful and determined have always contributed to prosperity. It is likely that the same will be true in the future. For example, after periods of decline due to historical exigencies, forceful and determined people were responsible for the prosperity that followed the Middle Ages, just as they were in Ancient Greece and after the fall of Roman Empire.

One can assess the strength of these sentiments by observing the energy and consistency with which wage earners pressed for the eight-hour work day. They remained united and loyal the world over and attained their goal without yielding. They ignored opponents trying to appeal to a "patriotic spirit of sacrifice." The workers looked ahead into the future and wanted to live better after the war than before. None of the workers called upon their comrades to work more for the advantage of capitalists, but many of the affluent ask their fellows to sacrifice for the good of the common man. In fact, some affluent people now preach the gospel of progressive taxation in order to support welfare for workers and for plutocrats. This is an obvious consequence of demagogic plutocracy. Both workers and capitalists have their scabs, but workers hate and persecute their scabs while members of the privileged class excuse theirs.

The masses, bolstered by the strength of their sentiments, managed to force the imposition of higher wages. Workers are not found busily inventing new forms of taxation to burden their own class, but there are affluent people who spend their time doing exactly that. What many people fail to understand is that revenue stolen from the treasury is, under present circumstances, stolen from enemies.

Common people perceive that those willing to go to extremes can be useful allies, even if workers are not themselves extremists. It is for this reason that Bolsheviks generally receive a sympathetic hearing from workers in all countries. The wealthy are too fragmented to oppose Bolshevism with an opposite extreme, for many are terrified upon hearing the word "militarism." Cicero was an apt representative of this position. He in fact failed to understand the dilemma posed by riots in the forum and the power of the Roman legions.

He honestly hoped, but in vain, for a government of noblemen sustained by the support of the people.

The popular classes are currently more powerful than the well-to-do. For this reason the bourgeois state is tottering, and the power of central authority is being eroded. Plutocracy is weakening, and demagogy is growing stronger. A downturn in the cycle is on its way. However, we cannot forecast its exact timing or magnitude.

As already pointed out, we will refrain from judging the desirability or undesirability of the facts noted above. Instead, we merely want to use these facts as empirical indicators of shifts in sentiment within opposing classes.

We began with an examination of empirical events and drew some inductions. What emerges is a general theory of social change. It seems likely that we have obtained worthwhile insights about the transformations through which societies move.

Notes

This paper was originally published on July 20, 1920, in *Rivista di Milano*.
1. See *Treatise on General Sociology* (1767ff., 2083).
2. In the House of Commons on June 8, Lloyd George sought to justify his change of position regarding the Soviet Union. He left moral considerations aside as he made his point: "If England did not care to negotiate with people guilty of atrocities, it should not have engaged in commercial relations with cannibals. But England has had more relations with cannibals than any other nation on earth."

    Lloyd's argument is in some sense defensible, although the company of cannibals does not seem to be a suitable location from which to act "in defense of law and justice." Many statesmen adopted Lloyd's position but without being honest enough to advertise it publicly.
3. The contrasts we will discuss here correspond to Class IV residues of sociality and Class V residues of integrity discussed in *Treatise on General Sociology*. Sentiments of hate which played such an important role in World War I are relevant at this point.

    The social world is heterogeneous. There are subcultures, general societies, and there is humanity as a whole. Subcultures act toward the general society in the same way that individuals do. They defend their own integrity while partly sharing and partly influencing sentiments of the society at large.

    In *Treatise on General Sociology* we observed certain laws (or uniformities) as they related to residues. If we were proceeding deductively from these laws, the order of the chapters in *The Transformation of Democracy* would be inverted. We would begin by discussing oscillations in general, and then the oscillations in sentiment under examination here, and finally "The Crumbling of Central Authority" as a special case.

    But at this stage a deductive track would be artificial. It would be wiser to employ that approach at a later date after further studies have strengthened the foundations of the theory. In the meantime it is useful to continue following the inductive approach attempting to confirm our initial conclusions.

4. This play was written by Vittorio Bersezio in 1902. It relates the life story of a harassed government clerk. Pareto implies that by 1920 civil servants had forgotten that their task was to serve rather than abuse the public.[Ed.]
5. Aristotle, *Politics* (V, 7, 19, 1310). We refer to the oligarchs identified by Theophrastus, *The Characters* (XXVI).
6. Aug. Thierry, *Essai sur l'histoire de la formation et des progrès du Tiers Etat*, p. 153.
7. Muratori, *Dissertazioni sopra le antichita italiane* (Rome, 1790), Vol. 3, Sect. 1, Diss. 52.
8. The fact that this principle has been observed in England and rejected in France explains, in part, why the monarchies of those two nations were to experience different destinies in the eighteenth century. Alexis de Tocqueville, in *L'Ancien Régime et la révolution*, p. 147, informs readers that "in the fourteenth century the maxim that 'the unwilling should not be taxed' was as firmly entrenched in France as in England herself. People remember that to violate this maxim was considered an act of tyranny, and to comply with the maxim was to do what was right." The opposite now seems to be true. "At the time there were a host of analogies between our political institutions and those of the English. But when national destinies part company, dissimilarities grow." We now see patterns beginning to converge again. [This is Pareto's translation of Tocqueville.]
9. *Memoirs* (Paris: Hachette), Vol. 7.
10. "When the king first raised taxes by his own authority he understood that the burden could not fall directly upon the nobles, for the latter formed a rival and dangerous class which would have rejected taxes detrimental to its own interest. So the king levied a tax from which nobles were exempt. . . . But as the needs of the public treasury grew with the functions of central power, the system of taxation expanded, diversified, and increased tenfold. Exploitative duties were then leveled on the nobles" (Tocqueville, p. 149). If one considers the progressive income tax and replaced the term "noble" with "well-to-do" Tocqueville provides a precise description of contemporary events. Parallel developments can be observed in the history of the Greek republics.
11. Trimalcione was the protagonist in *Satyricon* by Petronius. He was uneducated, rude, and very rich.[Ed.]
12. Only one conclusion can be drawn from available statistics. Aristotle reached this conclusion himself. Wealth measured in some monetary unit is not the same thing as wealth measured in economic goods. Poor King Midas learned this lesson too late.
13. Fustel de Coulanges summarizes these effects in *Les Transformations de la royauté pendant l'époque Carolingienne* (p. 665). "It was at the very moment that the monarchy was engaging in excesses of power that centralized control was shattered."

5
Appendix

Chapters of *The Transformation of Democracy* were published in serialized form between May 20 and July 20, 1920. Current events prove the prophetic nature of those chapters. These confirming events have come even earlier than I would have predicted. In turn, verification of the deductions presented in the earlier chapters of this monograph establishes the accuracy of my broader theory set forth in *Treatise on General Sociology*. Since *Treatise on General Sociology* was written, actual events have followed along something like a continuous curve, just as predicted. It appears that this curve will extend itself into the future, allowing us to forecast unfolding events before they occur.

It would be a laborious and even a useless exercise to list all of my predictions that have come true. After all, taken individually, these events are not very important. Only the overall pattern is important.[1] However, it will be useful to recall a few of these predictions and to employ them as specimens that enable us to plot the flow of the continuous curve of social history. We will proceed, as far as is possible, by using witnesses who are hostile to our case or at least who are unfamiliar with our theories.

Chapter 1 establishes that constant underlying forces outweigh superficial forces in determining the course of events. Politicians and lay people pay almost exclusive attention to superficial forces. It is for this reason that the programs they design to alter cyclical change have always failed, for those programs are aimed at superficial manifestations rather than underlying dynamics.

Very noticeable examples are to be found in government artifices for stabilizing the value of currency. We will consider a recent episode in the passages that follow.

Since July 8 of this year there has been a legal "conspiracy among plutocrats" afoot. Their aim is to strike at the government by lowering the exchange rate and causing a currency devaluation. The Honorable Mr. Giolitti was loudly cheered when he told Parliament on July 22 that "the people who try to influence political life with the billions they earned during the war are definitely in the wrong." But it is not clear whether he really believed what

74 The Transformation of Democracy

he said or merely believed that it was in the national interest to express that view publicly. The Honorable Mr. Modigliani, another scientific authority, expressed similar views. Many newspapers approved of their position, and magistrates began to act. According to one authority quoted in *Tribuna*: "We know that important investigations have been initiated, and the Royal District Attorney of Rome has begun criminal proceedings for fraud. Documents reveal that a number of stockbrokers are at fault. For example, in two days alone, nine million lire in state bonds were sold in a concerted effort to lower the rates. . . . Judicial inquiries will continue and they will extend to other cities." Inquiries have actually been conducted in Turin and Milan. But unfortunately, they had the life expectancy of soap bubbles. Despite their lofty intent the magistrates were unable to find cause for further legal action. Trends from the Geneva currency exchange and the Italian Stock Exchange are presented below.

Table 1: Shifts in Stock and Currency Values[2]

Corporate Units and Currency	July 22	July 30	October 23
Francs per 100 lire	32.15	31.60	23.82
Rendita 3.5%	72.75	71.50	66.70
Consolidee 5%	75.75	74.75	68.70
Banca Commerciale	980.	965.	995.
Credito Italiano	672.	667.	630.
Ferrovie Merid	443.	420.	326.
Rubattino	661.	662.	595.
Miniere Elba	227.	221.	132.
Acciaierie Terni	770.	760.	545.
Breda	217.	206.	173.
Ansaldo	179.	167.	108.
Ilva	148.	140.	98.
Fiat	279.	271.	188.

Little needs to be said. It would be ludicrous to say that government policies had desirable results! But since lessons of the past do not prevent policymakers from repeating mistakes, there is little reason to suppose that this most recent lesson will be heeded. The populace fails to understand societal events in scientific terms. And for that matter, so do most university professors.

Let us turn our attention to general socioeconomic trends. The Honorable Mr. Giolitti's Senate speech on September 26, 1920, provides a description that is basically sound, although tainted somewhat by the derivations that practical men are so prone to utilize.

Despite those derivations he provides readers with an account that is accurate in its general outline:

> The Fourth Estate was developing rapidly in Italy by the end of the last century.[3] [This is one of the developments comprising recent patterns of social change described in *Treatise on General Sociology*.] We remember that attempts to stop its ascending movement had deleterious consequences. [Of course, "good" needs to be defined because it can mean anything. For the Honorable Mr. Giolitti "good" means efficacious. His recent attempts to "restore state authority" have not been efficacious, but we will let others decide if they were "good" or "bad."] These social movements can be regulated and directed but they cannot be absolutely prevented.

To be theoretically precise he should have said: "These social movements can be modified slightly. But preventing such movements would be difficult indeed. It would require either changing the sentiments and interests of the majority or forcefully imposing a new order which would work on those sentiments and interests. Such forceful imposition would be difficult to achieve. Conditions such as those which enabled Octavian Augustus to rule as an absolute dictator are very rare." If the term "impossible" is used without the necessary qualifications, it makes one believe in the intervention of fate, whereas change simply reflects the interdependence of societal conditions.

The Honorable Mr. Giolitti goes on to attribute the economic oscillation of 1901-02 to miserable salaries. He is clearly wrong, as is evidenced by the fact that an identical oscillation is now underway, and salaries are generally high and very high in some cases. But mentioning salaries does serve an end by legitimating strikes. Our goal is not to justify or condemn this state of affairs. We merely want to call attention to it. The speech then becomes more interesting:

> Industrial and agricultural salaries were making quick progress in the last years before the war. [Those were good years for the demagogic plutocracy. It was the ascending period of the crisis and is bound to be followed by descent.] The war came . . . It produced an almost dizzy spur accelerating prewar trends in the cycle. [This is very true. The waves of the cycle became shorter and more intense.] Moreover, the battle trench was a seedbed for propaganda. [It is for this reason that prolongation of the war was a grave mistake for the demagogic plutocracy. It would have been comparatively advantageous had peace been declared in 1917. But prolongation of the war caused damaging change in popular sentiments and interests.] Soldiers returning home did not find their fellow citizens engrossed in the solemnity of the moment or in the arduous task of sustaining the army. On the contrary, returning soldiers found the country engrossed in its own amusement. Such amusement should have been repressed but it never was.

Giolitti may be making two mistakes in the above passage. The lesser mistake is to regard sumptuary laws as effective. History demonstrates that such laws are ineffective. The greater of the mistakes is an omission. The Honorable Mr. Giolitti fails, at least explicitly, to take account of the fact that the demagogic plutocracy in Italy and elsewhere was only able to support the war by dint of deceit.

The deceit began when people in Italy were told that the war would be short and inexpensive. People in all the countries were deceived by tax levies that were scaled to be light at the time debt was incurred but to become heavier each successive year. This was accomplished through government borrowing, government bond issues, and fictitious prosperity. Prosperity was the principal concern of all the people supporting the war, including profiteering sharks, honest producers, and wage earners. The sharks and those who profited from the war supported its continuation. Had it been otherwise, the war would never have lasted. And although there is now a pretense of prosecuting some of those sharks, no one questioned their actions during the war.

"During this period the political parties outdid one another in making vague and grandiose promises. They talked a lot about giving land to peasants and turning over factories to returning soldiers. These were just empty words as far as the politicians were concerned, but the downtrodden hearing these promises believed that they were acquiring new rights." The Honorable Mr. Giolitti is absolutely right. But it should be added that politicians have continued to make such promises in the aftermath of the war. Even His Honor Mr. Giolitti believes in a number of these promises.

Here is a list of some of the more absurd and impossible promises still being made.[4] The majority will be able to consume more and work less. Increased prosperity can be achieved while engaging in a war that destroys wealth. The prosperity of the masses can be supported by taxing the excess wealth of the rich. All this can be done without damaging future productive capacity. Production will be stimulated by innumerable fiscal tricks and whimsical measures designed to manipulate the economy. Production can also be maintained at the same time that we exhaust private capital, and without constituting socialist capital to replace it. Prosperity will be maintained despite the rise of shop committees, continued strikes, goldbricking at work, disregard for personal safety, and worker takeovers of factories, ships, and land, which threaten the integrity of personal property. States continue to pay interest on the enormous debts they have already contracted or are now contracting, and these debts will be paid with real rather than worthless currency. Governments gain the prosperity they long for by sinking deeper and deeper into a mire of debts and destruction of wealth. Indeed, prosperity under these conditions would be a miracle. People in search of such a miracle can only entrust their faith to some metaphysical entity like the sacred National Destiny, holy Democracy, holy Progress, or the divine Proletariat. Of course, proletarians say the only reason they failed to bring prosperity to Russia was because of the invidious spectre of satanic capitalism.

Such assertions are absurd because they negate the factual truth. They belong to the same class of falsehood and deception politicians used to manipulate public opinion during the war, and continue to use now that peace is here. On the other hand, such assertions can be useful and necessary for tactical reasons. They can be used to lead people along a path they would not follow by themselves. They can be used to mobilize partisans, to deflect the energy of adversaries, or to deceive the stupid people who have not yet taken a position. Promising people property is a particularly effective way of inciting them into action. Using enticements can also appease those who are less bold among one's adversaries so that they will detach themselves from the aggressive actions of their more militant fellows. Promising a great deal more than one intends to deliver has always been a great governing strategy. In addition, allowing domineering overlords to have a free hand can be a useful way of fomenting sentiments of resistance among the oppressed. Therefore, they support the government when it finally does intervene on behalf of the downtrodden to put a stop to the evil deeds it previously tolerated and favored. There are people who live in a state of sluggishness and who wake up only if they are beaten. There are also people who take pleasure in opposing the government. Yet they expect to be protected by that government. They try to enjoy a double advantage by professing socialism while entrusting the government to protect citizens against the deleterious consequences of socialism. These people have a change of heart when the government ceases to protect their personal interests, but by that time it can be too late.

Such popular sentiments impose one set of manifest goals and a different set of hidden goals upon the government. These involve policies that one implements but does not advertise. Certainly, even those government partisans who do not believe such lies must endeavor to conceal them. And a regime's adversaries cannot expose a government for promising what the adversaries want, even if the adversaries feel better equipped to make good on those promises.

Whether government programs will have useful or noxious consequences will be determined with the passage of time. It is difficult to make absolute judgements about the things a statesman says and does. Actions should be assessed contextually.

One cannot condemn a government solely because its actions are inconsistent with certain theoretical principles that have been confirmed by experience. On the other hand, it is necessary to determine if the measures adopted were the best options available to government functionaries. Recognition of this fact is written between the lines of the Honorable Mr. Giolitti's speech. Perhaps he could have been no more explicit. This would not have been in his interest or in the national interest.

It follows that our analysis treats statements primarily as derivations rather than as the literal truth. We will say it explicitly when these derivations reveal the real reasons for action. Consider the analysis that Giolitti offers:

> During the war a number of large industries were established. Everyone agreed that they were necessary, but these firms were not operating under open market conditions. The government was their only customer and this customer helped

> raise capital, supplied raw material, and paid whatever price was asked for finished goods. Under these conditions the industrialists saw no reason to quibble with workers over wages during the war. Costs were simply passed on to the government. As a result, postwar salaries have not kept pace with war salaries, particularly if one adjusts for inflation. It is important to keep in mind that high salaries during the war were not really paid by the industrialists.[5] Industrialists always conceded to the demands of the workers and for a good reason. If workers demanded 10 percent then the industrialists passed on a 20 percent price increase to the government.

Very good! There is nothing here to discuss. But there is something to add. The Honorable Mr. Giolitti describes one particular and extreme case of demagogic plutocracy in action. I set forth a more general treatment of this phenomena in *Treatise on General Sociology*, and we can now see it at work all around us. I will mention only one case. Those industrialists who betrayed their class interests by willingly accepting the imposition of an order to settle the metallurgical conflict shared the motives of industrialists described by His Honor Giolitti. The same motives induced bankers to offer pecuniary assistance to strikers who had taken over factories. Bankers certainly did not hope to be repaid by strikers, but they did expect assistance from a government grateful to have the strike concluded.

Readers are free to assess whether these facts and other current events are consistent with the predictions made in *Treatise on General Sociology* and in chapter 3 of this work. "Regardless of the time or place, we find plutocracy capable of turning desperate conditions to its own advantage. It apparently yields to rival forces with wily plans devised for recouping losses and concessions made to strong opponents. It circumvents obstacles it cannot overcome directly."

They are now trying to do exactly the same thing by establishing workers' committees within factories, by "registering" shares of stock, etc. How long will such "fair play" last? Sooner or later this issue will be settled by force. One group will forcefully assume the capacity to make decisions, and the other group will obey.

Events in Italy confirm insights on the use of force which I arrived at in *Treatise on General Sociology* (2174). "To ask whether force ought to be used in a society, whether the use of force is or is not beneficial, is to ask a question that has no meaning. Force is used by those who wish to preserve certain uniformities as well as by those who wish to overstep those uniformities. Violence of the first group stands in contrast and opposition to the violence of the second group."

For the time being, submissive and weak rulers are opposed by violent adversaries. The adversaries have gained added strength from the cowardice of their opponents. Among the established elite only the nationalists seem courageous enough to act boldly.[6] But the nationalists are few and their following is small.

Appendix 79

It is clear that these facts have general causes. They are not peculiar either to a country or to a system of government. Moreover, there is continuity in the unfolding movement of events. One can forecast the future based on familiarity with the past.

We made predictions after the occupation of the Mazzonis' factories. In fact this occupation began a chain of events that the government was unable to control despite the creation of a new department for the purpose and despite its intention to "restore state authority." To the contrary, the functionaries of this new government department yielded to the overbearing manners of unionists, thus contributing to the further erosion of government power.

When Senator Dante Ferraris reprimanded His Honor Mr. Giolitti for failing to prevent occupation of the factory, Giolitti simply responded that he was continuing his predecessors' work, and that Dante Ferraris was among those predecessors.[7] This is just one of many cases in which the activities of statesmen are dictated and directed by the deep social forces of sentiments and interests.

A constant theme is reproduced over and over again in these different derivations. In fact, His Honor Mr. Giolitti reproduced a derivation discussed at great length in *Treatise on General Sociology* (e.g. 2147,f18) when he said "public servants should not use weapons. Let 'people' engaged in strikes and rebellion behave as they want. Hypothetically, if they were to commit some crime they would be judged in the courts. Police have only to bring them to court but summary execution is not the job of the police. The crimes we are discussing, or at least most of them, do not deserve the death penalty. Yet, if anyone were killed while skirmishing with the police they would, in effect, have received the death penalty."

The Honorable Mr. Giolitti tells us "the Attorney General has established that strikers actually committing crimes are being reported to judicial authorities." This is in connection with piracy in the port of Genoa. But what does he say about amnesty? "You cannot put 500,000 workers on trial, even if they did occupy factories. This is particularly true in view of the fact that the government seemed to condone their actions at the time. On the other hand, let us think only in terms of the law. Workers occupying factories are guilty of an offense." His Honor Mr. Giolitti chooses to ignore the presence of Red Guards. "But expulsion could only be accomplished with loss of life. This would in effect be implementing a death penalty. Would that punishment be proportional to the crime?"

This derivation begins to sound stale. It might be better to replace it at this time. But if people wanted to discuss the derivation they might observe that it can be taken to great extremes. "The death penalty has been abrogated in Italy. Therefore, since the use of force by police involves a risk of death to the suspect, force should never be used against criminals." If we get to the facts, we will discover that the reluctance of police to use force which risks "inflicting the death penalty" has encouraged leftists to arm the Red Guards, to institute people's courts, and to kill innocent civilians. Neither the derivation itself nor a trial for the assassins—"executioners" if one wants to use that euphemism—will restore life to the victims.

In addition to the aforementioned murders, two additional events are worthy of notice. On September 22, workers occupying the factories killed Sergeant Dore. Many other people have been wounded or unlawfully imprisoned by this group. Such facts help contrast the decline of state power with the ascent of another power.

It is for this reason that these facts must be added to those discussed earlier in this volume. According to an article in *La Stampa*, October 21, 1920:

> Mr. Chicco, who was arrested in Marseilles, said he worked as a blacksmith's assistant in the Perotti factory. Although he was not a union member he volunteered for the Red Guard when labor disputes broke out in Turin. His duty was to mount a guard in front of the Bevilaqua factory which had been seized by the workers. Manning a guard post along with Andrea Vincenti and Giuseppe Rossi on the evening of September 22, they stopped a person passing by whom they recognized as a jail guard. When he refused to produce identification they seized him, dragged him inside the factory, and subjected him to a forceful search. The guard was Ernesto Scimula of the New Jails incarceration center in Turin. Scimula was then taken to the third floor of the factory and tried by a group of male and female workers who had become owners of the day, at which time Chicco said his part had ended and he went down to eat. When he returned two hours later Scimula was gone and Chicco knew that the poor fellow had been condemned to death. He had been taken before a sort of a court which even had some women and girls among the jurors. After a summary trial he was condemned to be burned alive inside a blast furnace, but the blast furnaces were turned off and Scimula was taken to a back street and cowardly shot. Chicco . . . then heard that another young man, Mario Sonzini, had been arrested by the workers of another factory and killed in the same place at the same time.

On October 17, 1920 *La Stampa* carried a story titled *The Murder of Guards Sant'Agata and Crimi Near the Savigliano Shop*.

> It happened at 6:30 a.m. on September 23 when Giuseppe Sirma, Antonio Lombardi, and Luigi Sant'Agata of the Royal Guards were returning to their barracks after night duty at the Borgo Dora police station. . . . Sirma and Lombardi were riding their bikes, Sant'Agata was walking. When they arrived at the Dora train station the guards who were riding took the overpass and Sant'Agata decided to take the short cut over a footbridge. . . . Red Guards on lookout from the roofs of the Savigliano shops saw Sant'Agata on that footbridge and opened fire.

It is useless to remind readers that these strikers were the good people who the government left unmolested because it was afraid that they might be hurt resisting any effort to hinder their praiseworthy enterprise. The government was afraid that people might have been killed in a forceful encounter between strikers and police. I am struck with horror at the idea. The newspaper article continued:

> When he reached Lanso Street, Sant'Agata noticed that the Red Guards were following him and he was still being shot at, so he hid along the railroad and waited for an opportunity to escape unnoticed and return to his barracks. But more Red Guards armed with muskets came out to follow his tracks, helped by local women who were indicating his location. When he bolted and ran up the side of the embankment he was shot, seized upon, and dragged to Stadella Street. Still alive, they shot him again. [Sirma and Lombardi went to the barracks for help.] The marshal in command took ten men to Stradella Street where they were fired upon by workers in Savigliano's shops. The marshal and his men were compelled to seek shelter in a home on Lanzo Street but in the retreat Mario Crimi was struck by a bullet and died.

Let us now consider how the opposing parties assessed these events. We find one position expressed in *Avanti*, the Socialist Party's daily newspaper:

> If those young men and women did form a court and condemn a man to death, then they acted in unison as a class rather than as individual inhuman criminals. A class strikes to defend itself when it is exasperated. Such a class may not be fully aware, but it is led by a blind instinct of self-preservation.[8]

This position stands in contrast to an interview with a plutocrat.

> Workers recently assumed control over their factories. This was accomplished without bloodshed. [Without bloodshed? What does this bureaucrat think flowed through the veins of Dore, Crimi, Sant'Agata, Sonzini, Scimula, and many others?] The occupation was tolerated because of a bold government policy. The government wanted to encourage workers in their experiment in order that they might discover for themselves that their interests are inseparable from those of capital.[9]

They also discovered that it is impossible to burn people when the furnaces have been turned off.

In chapter 4, I set forth reasons why we can expect common people to persevere over the well-to-do. But comparing these newspaper stories suggests yet another reason, if we can move beyond the veils of derivations to underlying motives.

Many facts of minor importance serve to demonstrate how these new masters usurp judicial power. It will be enough to consider, for example, fines levied in the Ferrare area. A message published in *Il Tempo* on July 6, 1920, is illustrative:

> The union has warned you that deliberations in the meeting of June 6, 1920, resulted in a fine of 500 lire because you unloaded three wagons of hay coming from Veneto without informing the porters' organization. Remember that this fine must be paid before you can continue your harvest. [This sentence was

82   The Transformation of Democracy

not subject to appeal, and the first order was followed by a second in order to urge the guilty party to pay the fine.] You are hereby notified of the union's determination to charge you an additional 50 lire for every day you delay payment of your fine.

Analogous events are likely to occur when the government implements its *control* over the factories. This may even lead to transfer of property.

There are numerous signs that public sentiments are being transformed. For instance, the Trade Union Chamber in Bologna commandeered grapes and fixed its own price. Accused of usurping state sovereignty, the secretary of the organization responded:

> The workers' organizations will naturally want an inventory of wine stocks kept in private cellars and in the cellars of innkeepers and shopkeepers. Moreover, shipping wine out of the province without our approval will be forbidden. I will also take this opportunity to deny malicious reports that we are only concerned with wine. We will fix maximum prices for fuel, fabric, shoes, linen, clothes, enamel kitchen utensils, glass, china, and so on. The Provincial Commission has never before dared to establish maximum prices. Executive organs for implementing future decisions have been established on each block. And as for the province, League Committees will be useful. People attack us for enforcing regulations which have not yet been enacted into law, for intrusiveness of power, and for developing a state within a state. Why should this not be? Law is a matter of force.[10] We should take note of the introduction to Professor Orlando's book *Administrative Law*. If one says "force," one does not always refer to an external force which dominates.[11] One can also refer to the moral force which seeks the proper balance of social values reached through difficult experiments.[12]

It would be of little use to mention the numerous cases in which private lands, houses, and shops have been invaded since the serialized publication of the earlier chapters in this book. These events are all too well known. But it may be useful to discuss worker takeover of ships to demonstrate how the emerging power of labor intrudes into foreign policy. Until now governments have jealously guarded the preserve of foreign policy as an area over which they alone were sovereign.

We will ignore the case of the Cogne, which was captured and sent to Fiume. Even though freight on the ship was foreign, some people might argue that the affair was in all other respects a domestic matter. But the foreign policy implications were much more clear when the Federation of Sea Workers with the complicity of the Confederation of Labor captured three Russian ships in the port of Genoa. Seizure of the Drusba, Soglasie, and Tchernomoor happened when Nitti was prime minister. The Rodosto was seized later, when Giolitti was minister. Organized labor clearly overstepped its authority in this matter. But when judicial authorities defined the seizures as acts of piracy and ordered the culprits arrested, workers viewed the government action as a judicial infringement on their prerogatives as an emerging nexus of power.

The government initially took a firm position and was bold in its defense of judicial sanction against the workers, but this boldness evaporated under the threat of a general strike. The accused were set free. Now they know they can do whatever they wish to do and still go unpunished.

This case is exactly like the occupation of the Mazzoni factories when Nitti was minister. It was followed by a general occupation of shops when Giolitti was minister. Whether government officials want "to restore state authority" is largely irrelevant. State authority is overwhelmed when it confronts a more powerful force.

The Federation of Unions in Amsterdam, self-appointed heirs of the Holy Alliance, declared a boycott against Hungary on June 20 because it disapproved of Hungarian domestic policies. European governments resigned themselves. Although the boycott was finally cancelled in July because it had little effect on the Hungarians, failure to punish boycotters can only encourage similar moves in the future, just as in the case of takeover in the Mazzoni shops.

It is also remarkable that railroad workers supported the unionist foreign and home policy by refusing to haul certain freight. They also forced the abandonment of Vallona.

A problem presents itself under these circumstances. For several years we have been noticing a series of social changes which have been intensified because of the war. But will the overall pattern of change begin to subside or will it generally accelerate, with occasional starts and stops, along its present course? If current trends do subside, will there or will there not be a gradual extension of changes occurring in the nineteenth century? If trends do continue at this velocity in their present direction, we can predict that society will encounter insuperable obstacles.[13] These obstacles include reduced production and increased consumption. Either a new cycle will begin shortly, or a catastrophe will occur forcing a future change.

In order to solve this problem, it would be necessary to statistically analyze aggregate patterns of sentiment and to assess whether sentiments are themselves undergoing any change. Social science cannot yet [in 1920] do this with precision. Therefore, we can only reason roughly about more or less probable events.

Examples from the past suggest that the current pattern of change will subside. But although it is true that history can repeat itself, two important conditions have changed. First, in the past there was an enormous number of people whose sentiments were stable. These people were "conservative" and leaders took advantage of this class. For instance, the extension of suffrage mobilized a new form of support for "conservative" causes. British governments often operated in this way, as did Napoleon III in France and Bismarck in Germany. Italian statesmen recently attempted to do the same, but they failed because they were unaware of the deep changes in sentiments and interests produced by the war. Therefore, it is doubtful whether similar trials will be successful in other countries. The number of common people who are "conservative" in their basic inclinations has been greatly reduced. Consequently, they cannot be relied upon very much.

The second change is that countries once had a considerable reservoir of savings and wealth. This has now been largely exhausted thanks to government programs and policies. In the past, governments were able to make up for mounting expenditures by raising taxes, and they were able to raise taxes without appreciably reducing production. But because of the war, taxes have reached a high plateau. It will be difficult to exceed this limit without prompting a considerable reduction in productivity with a corresponding loss in gross tax receipts. The relationship between tax structure and productivity is demonstrated by the fact that increased taxation has been accompanied by currency devaluation in many nations. Governments are exhausting the sources from which they have been taking money to satisfy greedy partisans and to calm political opponents. Day by day, the burden grows. It will eventually reach a point beyond which the load will no longer be tolerated. This is how the political realm dominates the economic. This same pattern of events was responsible for the final ruin of the Roman Empire. The same thing could happen now.

However, one must also take account of the colonial exploitation of wide areas of Asia and Africa. This exploitation is of particular benefit to England, the United States, and France. It will not really benefit Italy, which must be content with crumbs that fall from the table of those other greedy eaters. A policy like the one adopted at the end of the Roman Empire, which allows the demagogy to have its way within a country under the supposition that domestic prosperity can be maintained via the exploitation of foreign territories, will fail countries like Italy. That kind of policy can only benefit the most successful colonial powers.

One question remains unanswered. How can one establish a balance between the two types of countries? Will they ever come into direct conflict? This might be one way in which the catastrophe could materialize. Afterward a new cycle would begin.

Notes

This chapter was begun in October and finished in early November, 1920, as an accompaniment to the four earlier chapters.[Ed.]
1. People who knowingly or unknowingly close their eyes to reality always say: "Everything will work out for the best. We must have confidence in our national destiny and in the good sense of people." Some people say this because they truly believe it and others because they want desperately to believe it.

   The sophism of the bald man is based on the same premise. You can pluck a hair from the head of a man with plenty of hair without making him bald. You can pluck

a second hair without making him bald, and so on. Some might, therefore, fallaciously reason that you can take away all of his hair without making him bald.
2. There is only one exception to the falling rates in Table 1. It is unclear what accounts for this exception.
3. The Fourth Estate refers to the political awakening the working class.[Ed.]
4. I wrote in greater detail on this subject in *Teorie e fatti* (Florence: Vallecchi, 1920).
5. The pliability of owners to workers demands is explained in *Treatise on General Sociology* (2187). "Many of them are speculators who hope to pass on the costs of strike concessions to consumers or to be relieved by government aid paid for by tax-payers." The Honorable Mr. Giolitti was surely too busy to read my book. But experience led him to the same conclusion. The facts thus provided confirmation for my theory.
6. "Government failure to alter the wheat policy, which prohibits sale of bread for more than three lire, is criminal and can be attributed to an impotent administration and a cowardly ruling class which imposes itself in a demagogic way. And the persistence of a compulsory workday of not more than eight hours is also criminal. . . . The nation is approaching economic collapse. Strong measures are necessary. Overtime has been successfully introduced in Germany and Belgium where the ten-hour day is needed in order to make up for lost productivity during a year of disorders, idleness, and work stoppage. This is the basis for the program of recovery we require. . . . But energy is needed in order to carry it out. Is there any reason to believe that the worn-out and impotent forces of democratic and liberal parliamentarianism, which are now in power, will have this energy?" *Idea Nazionale* (October 27, 1920).
7. Giolitti said in his speech that "the Mazzonis' firm, a very important company . . . locked out workers because it did not wish to accede to their demands. Workers then occupied the factories. This happened more than a year ago. What did the government do then? Senator Dante Ferraris was the head of the department in change. What a laugh that citizens viewing the hearings had over this! He failed to expel the strikers when he had a chance. He even acknowledged their takeover by sending in the government representative to manage the occupied factories. Is it possible that I followed his example for the six hundred factories in the metallurgical industry?" Mr. Giolitti's successors are likely to say the same thing. "Is it possible that I followed Ferraris's example by sending government representatives to the thousands of private establishments taken over by workers, or that I followed Giolitti's example by instituting 'controls' that no one wanted?" This demonstrates what people have known for centuries. Little thieves are punished while big thieves go free.
8. Cited in *Idea Nazionale* (October 24, 1920).
9. *Il Nuovo Giornale* (October 24, 1920).
10. People used to say that only "German barbarians" dared to assert that might makes right and force makes law. But now the divine proletariat adopts the same principle.
11. What is happening to the dogma of universal suffrage? Are the gods of democracy on the decline?
12. It is human nature to think that whatever state of affairs is to one's own advantage is also morally "right." We discussed this derivation at great length in *Treatise on General Sociology*. This passage appeared in *Il Resto del Carlino* (September 21, 1920).
13. Paolo Orano has written a very good article on this subject. It is titled "Il controllo operaio," *Pagine libere* (November 1, 1920).

Epilogue

Charles H. Powers

The Transformation of Democracy reveals Pareto's theoretical insights in their most dramatic splendor. A society is ruined when too many people hunger for easy money. Pareto begins with the premise that deep-seated value orientations determine peoples' proclivities for deceit and squandering the resources of others. Building on this premise, he concludes that a society in which people have forgotten how to work, and dream instead of growing rich through speculation or through legal maneuvering or political largesse, is a society which will impoverish itself. This is a story that would, Pareto feared, be replayed over and over again in history.

Pareto views Europe, circa 1920, in this light. Societies were dominated by conniving speculators who grew rich manipulating money and commodity markets and by having governments absorb indirect costs of production and assume burdens of risk in capitalist enterprise. At the same time, common people sought effective (and costly) social welfare programs and high wages. Pareto's analysis of Europe in the 1920s may in some ways be applicable to contemporary events in the Western industrial world. Pareto would not have been surprised at this, for he advanced his ideas in the context of a general theory applying to societies of all kinds and during all time periods.

The pursuit of general laws was a trademark of Pareto's work throughout his life. As an engineering student he mathematically described the elasticity of matter as a reflection of the moving equilibrium between countervailing forces of expansion and contraction. By the end of his life he was attempting to explain societal change with the same rigor and sophistication. He argued that the ebb and flow of historical events reflects the operation of inexorable laws governing opposition among countervailing forces of economic expansion and contraction, centralization and decentralization of power, and social inhibition versus relaxation of social control. Discovery of these laws would allow people to forecast social change.

88 The Transformation of Democracy

As a sociologist Pareto sought to identify the laws of social organization. Unfortunately, his contemporaries were unable to grasp the power of his theory. Yet, people are still reading, being informed by, and attempting to improve upon Pareto's basic insights and discoveries. It is hoped that this volume will serve to further the social scientific enterprise that Pareto began.

Index

Agrarian reform, 57, 60
Alexander the Great, 42
Ancient world, 26–27, 31, 57, 64
Anarchy, 34, 42, 46, 51
Aristotle, 29, 66
Arminius, 58
Articles of Kiersy, 44–45
Assize of Jerusalem, 50
Athens, 27, 64
Augustus, 57–58, 75
Austria-Hungary, 1, 3, 42, 59
Authority, 18–19, 34, 37, 44, 71, 79

Bakunin, Dina, 5
Barbarians, 38–39
Beatrice, 64
Behavior, 63–64, 77
Beliefs, 14–15, 63–64, 76
Benso, Camillo, 3
Biblical stories, 29
Bismarck, Otto Fürst von, 58, 83
Bobbio, Norberto, 9
Boccaccio, Giovanni, 64
Bolsheviks, 28, 50, 65, 70
Bolshevism, 27, 30, 59
Bourgeois, 42, 58; state, 51, 71
Bourgeoisie, 27, 34, 42, 47, 59, 68
Brentano, 39
Bureaucracy, 57, 64–65, 79
Business cycle, 12–13

Caesar, 57
Capet (king of France), 44
Capitalism, 40, 42, 51, 52, 76
Capitalists, 30–31, 66, 68, 78
Carolingian rule, 37, 42, 46

Cartesian philosophy, 3
Carthage, 57
Catholic Church, 44, 51, 52, 64
Cavour, Earl of, 3
Céligny, 9–10
Central Empires, 59
Centralization of power, 8, 13–14, 18, 37, 41–42, 45–46, 51, 59, 70. *See also* Decentralization of power
Centrifugal force, 13–14, 18, 37, 41–42, 45–46, 51, 56, 59, 71
Centripetal force, 13–14, 18, 37, 41–42, 45–46, 51, 56, 59, 70
Charlemagne, 42–43, 51
Charles Albert (of Savoy), 2, 48
Charles the Bald, 43, 45
China, 27
Christ, 27
Christian Science, 31
Christians, 31, 64
Cicero, 70
Circulation of elites, 8, 13–14, 87, 50, 57, 78
Civil servants, 45, 47, 65, 79
Class. *See* Middle class; Ruling class; Working class
Clemenceau, George, 28
Clergy, 66
Colonialism, 59
Combinations, 8–11, 56
Communalism, 37
Comte, Auguste, 11
Conference of Vienna, 2
Consensus, 56–57
Consequences of policies, 12–16, 31, 40, 60, 66, 68, 73–77, 83–84

89

90   The Transformation of Democracy

Conservatism, 14–15, 58–59, 83–84
Co-optation, 13, 20, 56, 66
Coulanges, Fustel de, 44
Craft gilds, 39
Crusades, 27, 31
Culture, 52, 65
Cyclical change, 9, 12–16, 18, 27, 29, 34, 37–38, 41–42, 48, 51, 56–57, 60, 71, 73, 75, 79, 83–84

Dante Alighiere, Duranto, 64
Darwin, Charles, 29
Darwinists, 33
Death penalty, 79–80
Decadence, 18, 20, 60, 64, 69, 75
Decentralization of power, 8, 13–14, 18, 34, 37, 41–42, 47, 51, 56, 59, 71. *See also* Centralization of power
Democracy, 18–19, 25, 27, 30, 40–41, 56, 64, 76
Democratization, 55, 83
Depretis, Agostino, 48
Derivations, 9–11, 26, 28–29, 32, 38, 40, 44, 50, 56, 58–59, 63–64, 74, 76–77
Devaluation of currency, 68, 73–74, 76, 84
Disintegration, 42
Divine right, 31
Doria, Giorgio, 2
Dreyfus, Alfred, 58

Economic crisis, 12–13, 18–19, 29, 51, 57, 65, 68, 75–76, 84
Einstein, Albert, 21
Elections, 17, 58
Equilibrium, 4, 7, 11, 18, 37, 41–42, 63
Equilibrium of power, 30
Empiricism, 26, 31, 56, 63
Empiricists, 27, 39
England, 27, 30, 32, 40, 42, 48, 57, 59, 63, 83
Erosion of authority, 13–14, 18–19, 34, 37, 41–42, 44–45, 47, 50–51, 56, 59, 71
Estates-General, 50, 66
Evolution, social, 33, 38, 50
Experimental method, 25, 27–29, 33, 38

Faith, 11, 14–15, 27–28, 30–31, 51, 64. *See also* Catholic Church; Christians; God; Religion
Falch, 38
Falcioni, 60

Farmers, 57–58
Farmworkers, 56–58, 60, 65–66
Ferraris, Dante, 79
Ferrari, Giuseppe, 29
Feudalism, 31, 37–39, 42, 44, 46–47, 49–51, 64
Fiefdoms, 39
Florence, 4–5, 64
Forecasting events, 32, 37, 60, 63, 71, 73, 79, 84
Force, 13, 20, 56–57, 78–79, 82. *See also* Centrifugal force; Centripetal force
Foxes, 8, 13–14
France, 1, 37, 44, 46–47, 50, 58–59, 66–68, 83–84
Free trade, 5–6, 40
French Revolution, the, 27–28, 50
Franco-Prussian War, the, 58
Functionalism, anti-, 28

Geneva, 10, 74
Genoa, 1–2, 79
Germany, 32, 38, 42, 55, 58–59, 83
Gilds, 33, 39, 67
Giolitti, Giovanni, 73–79
God, 64
Good government, 29–30
Government: manipulation of, 18, 60, 68–69, 73–76, 78; -spending, 50, 60, 67–69, 76, 78
Gracchi brothers, the, 57, 60
Greece, 57
Greed, 42
Group persistence, 8–9, 11
Guerin, 47

Hegel, Georg Wilhelm Friedrich, 30
Hegira, 27
Historical method, 33
Holly Roman Empire, 43
House of Commons, 32, 40, 43, 50
Howell, George, 39
Humanitarianism, 51, 64
Hypocrisy, 64

Ideology, 14–15, 40, 44, 50–51, 64, 76–77
Ideals, 27
Immunity, 45–46
Imperial benefices, 38
Imperialism, 42, 51, 59, 64
Inalienable rights, 31

Income distribution, law of, 7, 60
Industrialization, 40
Inequality, 55
Interdependence, 3–4, 7, 11, 28–29, 63–64, 83
Interests, 19, 26, 28, 56–58, 60, 63, 65, 69, 75, 77, 79
Islam, 27
Isocrates, 64
Italy, 1–6, 17–21, 27, 43, 47–48, 58–59, 75–76, 83–84
Italian: unification, 4; republics, 66
Ivan the Terrible, 41, 57

Japan, 41
Jouhaut, 47
Juglar, Clement, 29

Kant, Immanuel, 64

Labor Party, 43
Landowners, 48, 56, 65–66
Laissez-faire economics, 5–6, 40, 60
Lanzillo, Agostino, 40
Latifundium, 60
Lausanne, 7, 9–10
League of Nations, 30, 64
Legitimation, 56
Lenin, Vladimir Ilich, 27, 47, 57
Leningrad, 41
Liberalism, 15
Liberty, 40
Liguria, 2
Lions, 8, 13–14
Lloyd George, David, 43
Logical-experimental science, 26–29, 33–34, 52
Lombardy, 2, 29
Louis XIV, 50
Louis XV, 50

Maine, Sumner, 25
Manipulators, 18, 50, 56, 60, 66–67, 69, 73–75, 77–78
Mario, 57
Marx, Karl, 30, 51
Marxists, 51
Mattenier, Marie, 2
Mazzini, Giuseppe, 2, 48
Mazzoni brothers, the, 48–50, 79, 83
Merovingian rule, 37, 39

Metaphysics, 26, 28–30, 33, 63
Middle Ages, 33, 37, 39, 41–42, 45–47, 50–52, 57
Middle class, 65
Milan, 74
Militarism, 6, 22, 40, 42, 57–59, 68, 70
Military: class, 55; control, 57; technology, 30
Mill, John Stuart, 30
Miseries of Travet, 65
Missi dominici, 43
Modigliani, 74
Mohammed, 27
Monarchy, 41–42, 45, 50, 67–68
Montesquieu, Charles de, 38
Muratori, Lodovico, 66–67
Muslims, 27, 64
Mussolini, Benito, 22
Myths, 40, 44

Napoleon, 2
Napoleon III, 57, 83
Nationalists, 78
Negative effects. *See* Positive and negative effects
Newton, Isaac, 21, 33, 63
Nitti, Francesco, 82–83
Nobility, 66–67, 71
Non-logical action, 9, 11, 57. *See also* Sentiments
Norman invasion, 42
Norms, 15

Oligarchy, 41, 66
Olivetti, A.O., 41
Opinions, 63, 65, 76
Orlando, Vittorio, 82
Oscillations, 12–16, 18, 29, 37–38, 41–42, 48, 51, 56–57, 60, 71, 73, 75
Owners of factories, 48–50, 66, 78

Padua, 47
Pagans, 64
Pantaleoni, Maffeo, 6–7, 10
Pareto family, the, 1–3
Paris, 2
Parliamentary government, 30, 40, 42, 48, 56
Parsons, Talcott, 11
Particularism, 37
Patriotism, 58, 64–65

Peasants, 60, 65, 76
Persistence of aggregates, 42, 56
Pertile, Antonio, 38
Peruzzi family, the, 5
Piedmont, 1, 3, 48
Pisa, 64
Plutocracy, 18–19, 34, 42, 51, 55–60, 65, 67, 71, 73, 75, 78
Pobyedonostzev, Konstantin, 31
Polytechnic Institute of Turin, 3
Popolari, 60
Positive and negative effects, 28–29
Power. *See* Centralization of power; Decentralization of power; Royal power; Shattering of central power
Precarium, 38
Productivity, 18–19, 65, 69, 76, 84
Profit, 40
Profiteers, 69, 76, 78
Progressive taxes, 30, 32
Proletarian, 30, 52, 65, 70
Proletariat, 52, 64–66, 76
Propaganda, 55, 76
Property rights, 66, 76–77
Prussia, 58

Railway employees, 45–47, 83
Rationalism, 28
Rationalization, 45–46, 63
Red Guards, 79–81
Régis, Jane, 9–10, 22
Religion, 27, 29, 37, 41, 51–52, 63–65. *See also* Catholic Church; God; Faith
Rentier, 9, 57
Residues, 10–11, 34, 37, 56, 63
Rhetoric, 50
Ricci, Vincenzo, 2
Rich people, 66–69, 76
Rigola, 48–49
Rome, 31, 38, 42, 57–58, 60, 64, 70, 84
Rome Railway Company, 4
Roman Triumvirats, 28
Romulus, 27
Royal power, 39, 51, 57
Ruling class, 50, 69, 77–78
Russia, 41–42, 50–51, 57, 59, 76, 82
Russian Revolution, the, 28, 58–59
Russo-Japanese War, the, 58

Saint-Simon, 67
Saracen invasion, 42

Savers, 55, 60
Saving, 51, 83
Savoy, House of, 1, 3, 48
Scabs, 47, 66
Science, 3–4, 21–22, 29, 33–34, 63–64
Scientific: explanation, 4, 28; principles, 21–22, 33–34
Sedan, 58
Senecey, Baron, 66
Sentiments, 8–11, 14–15, 18, 20, 26, 28, 31–32, 34, 55–57, 59, 63, 65–70, 75, 77, 79, 83
Shattering of central power, 13–14, 18–19, 34, 37, 41–42, 44–45, 47, 50–51, 56, 59, 71
Skepticism, 10–11, 14–15, 20, 64
Smith, Adam, 5, 40
Social: change, 12–16, 21, 26–28; control, 65; system, 4, 11, 28–29, 75
Sociality, 37
Socialism, 40, 44, 51–52, 77
Socialists, 17, 30, 51
Sorel, Georges, 10, 40
Sovereignty, 19, 41–42, 44, 46, 50, 82–83
Soviet Union, 57, 66, 76, 82
Sparta, 27, 31, 64
Speculators, 9, 55–56, 59, 60, 68–69, 73–74, 76
Spitalfields silk weavers, 40
Stratification, 55
Strikes: agricultural, 43, 48; labor, 17, 30, 66, 75, 78–83
Subjugation, 41
Subsidies, 60, 68–69, 78
Sulla, Lucius, 57

Tastes, 28
Taxation, 32, 60, 67–69, 76, 84
Third International, 27, 51
Tolstoy, Leo, 47
Traditional attachments, 37
Traditionalism, 14–14, 42
Travet, 65
Transformation, societal, 12–19, 25, 29, 33, 41, 44, 56, 60, 66, 71
Treatise on General Sociology, 9–18, 25–27, 34, 37–38, 40, 56–58, 73, 75, 78–79
Trimalcione, 69
Triple Entente, 59
Tsarist autocracy, 31, 57, 59

Turin, 3, 49, 74
Turkey, 22, 59
Tuscany, 1, 65

Uniformity, desire for, 37
Unions, 6, 39, 83, 41, 43–50, 52, 79
United States, 59, 84
Usurpation, 49
Utopia, 64

Varus, General, 58
Vasalage, 38
Vested interests, 18–19

Vico, Giovanni, 29, 38
Violence, labor, 79–81

Walrus, Leon, 7
War indemnity, 32
Webb, Beatrice, 39–40, 44
Webb, Sidney, 39–40, 44
Wilson, Woodrow, 30, 32
Working class, 6, 30–32, 55–56, 64–67, 70–71, 77
World War I, 17, 22, 30, 40, 42, 48, 51, 55, 59, 58, 68–69, 75–76, 78